BOY
NEXT
DOOR

Books published by The Ballantine Publishing Group
are available at quantity discounts on bulk purchases
for premium, educational, fund-raising, and special
sales use. For details, please call 1-800-733-3000.

BOY NEXT DOOR

THE JAMES VAN DER BEEK STORY

Alex Tresniowski

BALLANTINE BOOKS • NEW YORK

A Ballantine Book
Published by The Ballantine Publishing Group
Copyright © 1999 by Alex Tresniowski

This is an independent work and is not authorized in any way by James Van Der Beek.

All rights reserved under International and Pan-American Copyright Conventions. Published in the United States by The Ballantine Publishing Group, a division of Random House, Inc., New York, and simultaneously in Canada by Random House of Canada Limited, Toronto.

Ballantine and colophon are trademarks of Random House, Inc.

www.randomhouse.com/BB/

Library of Congress Catalog Card Number: 99-90547

ISBN 0-345-43672-5

Manufactured in the United States of America

First Ballantine Book Edition: September 1999

10 9 8 7 6 5 4 3 2 1

For Gracie & Zach & Willie & Emily,
the best kids in the whole world

Contents

A Fateful Day

One of the six major moments in his life was about to happen, and James Van Der Beek didn't have a clue. He was only thirteen—nine years younger than he is today—and several inches shorter than his current six-foot frame. But he had the same tousled blond hair, the same sensitive blue eyes, the same sheepishly engaging smile—and the same intense love for the game of football.

So there was James—or as his fellow eighth graders and coaches called him, Beek—playing football in gym class in his hometown of Cheshire, Connecticut. He was happily dashing up and down the field, as he had a thousand times before, oblivious to the nasty trick that fate was about to play on him. All he could think was how much he liked playing football, and how much he'd love to play professionally when he got older.

It was a dream a million skinny kids in shoulder pads across the country liked to dream. But to young James, it didn't seem far-fetched at all. He

1

had excellent speed, good instincts, and, most important, a passion for playing. He was shaping up to be a nifty junior high school running back. So what if he was a little small for the game, and not likely to ever have a big enough body for football? If he worked hard each and every day, why couldn't he buck the odds and become a pro someday?

Those were the positive thoughts in Beek's head on that fateful day, at least until he saw a football thrown in his direction. Then he had only one thought—catch it. But as he jumped in the air to grab the pass, there was a crunching collision, and suddenly James was sprawled on the ground, out cold. When he got up, something was wrong—he felt dizzy, light-headed, not sure of where he was. Later, he was examined, and the doctor delivered his diagnosis: James had suffered a mild concussion, and he would not be able to play tackle football again that year.

It was the best thing that ever happened to James Van Der Beek.

Sidelined for the season, he had to find something else to do. That something else turned out to be acting. To keep himself busy while his buddies were banging on the football field, he auditioned for the lead role of Danny Zuko in a local production of *Grease*. He got the part and, more important, he caught the acting bug.

And now, a mere nine years later, James Van Der Beek—all of twenty-two years old—is a major TV and movie star, on the verge of full-blown superstardom.

His smart and nuanced portrayal of sixteen-year-old Dawson Leery, the sensitive Steven Spielberg wannabe and lead character on the WB series *Dawson's Creek*, has helped turn the show into a major hit for the fledgling network—it's perhaps the most important and groundbreaking series aimed at teens and preteens ever aired on TV. While all of James's young costars—Joshua Jackson, Katie Holmes, and Michelle Williams—have become big celebrities in their own right, it is James who has established himself as the show's breakout star. The *Denver Post*, for example, singled him out and called him "one of the most photogenic young actors to emerge recently on the small screen." Just check out any of his dozens of adoring fan Web sites, or recall his amazingly accomplished and self-parodying appearance in 1999 as the host of *Saturday Night Live*, and you'll know he's the real deal, a bona fide candidate for pop-culture-icon status—and one of the very best bets, among all the many young TV stars, to be around long, long after his current show is gone.

On top of all that, Beek also recently starred in the hit football movie *Varsity Blues*, guiding the film to a surprisingly boffo box-office take of nearly $50 million in just five weeks—proof that James also has the potential to become one of Hollywood's most bankable leading men. "He has a tremendous focus and intensity that remind me of a young Tom Cruise," says Patrick Read Johnson, the director who discovered James and cast him in the actor's first movie, *Angus*, in 1990. "He doesn't pick the lint off his pants or look at the floor when he talks to you—he looks you right in the eye. And that's a tremendously engaging quality."

It's an appeal that goes far beyond Beek's teen-idol looks, though there's no denying that his handsome, preppy features look great on the silver screen. The soft and riveting baby-blue eyes, the lively and expressive eyebrows, the square jaw and the solid cheekbones, and, of course, the playful, aw-shucks grin—it all adds up to the kind of movie-star face that makes his fans go weak. After all, this is the guy his *Dawson's* costar Joshua Jackson referred to as "Captain America."

But what separates James from the other pretty boys in Hollywood is a particular quality he projects in whatever role he plays: an honesty, an earnestness, a complete and total believability. "He's obviously a good-looking guy, which is why so many teens love him," says Mitchell Lawrence, the excellent character actor who played James's film teacher in the first season of *Dawson's Creek*. "But there's something very accessible about his looks, too, and that's what draws younger kids and older people to him. He's a completely honest guy, and that's what I really like about him. He doesn't seem to have a different agenda when he's working than when he's not. And the more that honest quality shines through, the more powerful an actor he'll become."

Patrick Read Johnson agrees, though he's more intrigued by a different quality. "James is not classically handsome, he's kind of interestingly handsome," says Johnson, who still keeps in touch with his pal and would love to do another film with him. "There's a lot of intelligence at work there, and a lot of warmth and politeness, but there's something more than that. Like Tom Cruise, he's the all-American guy, but what makes him interesting is that, if you scratch the surface, you'll find pain, anger, frustration, all this stuff. There is more to James than meets the eye, and that's the quality that makes someone a movie star."

It could be argued that James is merely riding a remarkable cultural wave—the phenomenal explosion of teen-oriented entertainment. With new networks like Fox, the WB, and UPN needing hours and hours of fresh programming, TV producers tapped into a rich market that had never really been catered to before: teenage and preteen viewers. Shows stocked with young and unknown actors were cheap to produce; just as important, they were good bets to attract the kinds of viewers that advertisers craved. But few could have predicted the mind-boggling success that shows aimed at teens would enjoy.

It started with the youth brigade of *Beverly Hills*

90210. That show's durability and appeal to young viewers opened the floodgates to a host of similar programs: *Party of Five, Buffy the Vampire Slayer, Felicity*, and, of course, *Dawson's Creek*, to name a few. Suddenly Hollywood's hottest new stars were barely out of high school.

The next step, naturally, was movies, and a host of TV stars made the leap to the silver screen. *Party of Five*'s Neve Campbell went on to make the hip horror flicks *Scream* and *Scream 2*; her *Party* costar Jennifer Love Hewitt scored big in *I Know What You Did Last Summer* and its gory sequel. *Buffy*'s Sarah Michelle Gellar sparkled in *Scream* and *Cruel Intentions*, while practically the entire cast of *Dawson's Creek* parlayed their TV fame into movie roles—Joshua Jackson in *Urban Legend* and *Cruel Intentions*, Michelle Williams in *Halloween: H2O*, Katie Holmes in *Disturbing Behavior*, and James Van Der Beek in *Varsity Blues*.

All of these young actors are bright and gifted artists with clearly promising futures. By most accounts they are also all remarkably dedicated to their craft and intent on making smart career moves. Unlike the Brat Pack of the 1980s, which ruled for a few years in popular movies before burning out in a blaze of lousy films and bad attitudes, the current crop of levelheaded stars seems likely to be around for a while.

But of all the promising and marketable young actors working today, James Van Der Beek clearly stands out. He has shown a willingness to play against type in all of his movies, not just settle for a variation on his TV character. He has also demonstrated a strong desire to stretch his talents whenever he can. He seems equally adept at playing serious drama (his second film, *I Love You, I Love You Not*, was about the Holocaust) and at goofy comedy (his *Saturday Night Live* performance was polished and assured). He also has an extensive background in the theater, the sort of training that makes him a dream for directors to work with. James looks like he's a single, juicy role away from shedding his TV trappings and becoming a full-fledged movie star.

That role could be the much-coveted part of Anakin Skywalker, the young Darth Vader, in one of the hotly anticipated upcoming *Star Wars* prequels. The Internet is buzzing with rumors that director George Lucas will offer the amazing part to James, and in so doing effectively anoint him the brightest young star of his generation. "James would be phenomenal in the role," says Johnson. "The young Darth Vader has to be this incredibly charismatic character, and I think James would bring this sympathetic and noble quality to him. All George Lucas has to do is meet James and look into his eyes, and he'll immediately say, 'Yep, this is Anakin Skywalker.'"

Johnson's point is well taken: part of James's appeal is that he can communicate so much with so little. To watch him on *Dawson's Creek* is to feel that, somehow, you know him. He has an easy familiarity that draws people to him and makes them feel they're in the presence of a friend. Although I personally have never met or talked to James, and although I didn't interview him for this book, I also feel that, somehow, I know him. Interviewing several producers and directors who have had the good luck to work with James over the years—and who couldn't say enough nice things about him—confirmed what I had suspected about James from reading up on his life. On top of being a top-notch actor, he is also a top-notch person—a world-class nice guy.

Hard to believe that someone teetering on the brink of global megastardom can still be a regular Joe, but, sure enough, Beek is. Take, for instance, his apartment in Wilmington, North Carolina, where he films *Dawson's Creek*. It isn't filled with pricey gadgets and trendy furniture—the kinds of things that would lead you to believe that his heart-throb status has gone to his head. Instead, it's packed with tasteful, understated, regular-guy stuff. Nor does Beek—who last year was named one of *People* magazine's 50 Most Beautiful People—spend a lot of time fussing with his wardrobe or his hair. His beauty routine? "I basically jump in the shower, throw a hat on, and take it off at work," James told *People*. "In half an hour, my hair is cool." As for the baseball cap he favors, "I'm ambidextrous," he reported. "I wear it both ways, but on formal occasions, brim forward."

Can this cool and ultracasual dude really be the next big thing? Can someone the world hadn't heard of two years ago become a household name just like that? Can this totally perfect guy actually be for real? You bet he can, and it's all thanks to that fateful concussion—potentially the most famous bump on the head in Hollywood history.

The question is—who exactly is James Van Der Beek, and where the heck did he come from?

CHAPTER ONE

The Connecticut Kid

There is much about James Van Der Beek that makes him stand out, not the least of which is his distinctive name. It takes a while to get used to, and it's more likely to be mispronounced than a name like, say, Brad Pitt. Even today, in the midst of his speedy ascent into the upper ranks of American actors, James occasionally encounters people who have trouble with his name—and that includes his own employers, Columbia TriStar, the folks behind *Dawson's Creek*. Recently, "they sent me a gift," Beek recalled, "addressed to James Van Der *Horn*."

Get it straight, America: it's Van Der *Beek*, which is Dutch for "by the brook" (funny how the guy with a creek named after him is actually named for a brook!). Sure enough, James grew up in just the kind of bucolic serenity his name suggests. He and his younger brother Jared (now nineteen) and his younger sister Juliana (now seventeen) were raised in the quiet and woodsy Connecticut suburb of Cheshire, in a modest split-level home that was "not as big as Dawson's," James told *Teen People* (his TV counterpart lives in a sprawling house in a seaside New England town, a fictional location that shares a quaintness and upper-middle-class prosperity with James's real hometown).

James was born on March 8, 1977. That makes him a Pisces, one of the more complex and interesting astrological signs. Pisces tend to be imaginative and sensitive, compassionate and kind, intuitive and sympathetic—all traits that seep through James's portrayal of Dawson Leery. People born under the sign of Pisces are also typically gentle, patient, generous, and good-natured, and their easygoing, affectionate natures make them popular with different kinds of people (this, too, sounds like James, who would eventually travel comfortably between the disparate worlds of sports and theater).

The flip side to these admirable qualities is that some Pisces are weak-willed and malleable, more concerned with the problems of others than with their own. Because of this they can be easily misled in relationships and end up on the wrong side of breakups. They react instinctively rather than intellectually and, though they want to be recognized for their creativity, often disappear into dreamworlds and end up being labeled impractical. All of these negative traits sometimes turn up in the character of Dawson Leery, an aspiring filmmaker who often seems to exist on a different

Just the Facts

James's Birth Date: March 8, 1977
Birthplace: Cheshire, Connecticut
Height: 6 feet
Weight: 190 lbs.
Hair: dark blond
Eyes: brown
Parents: Melinda and Jim
Siblings: brother Jared (three years
  younger) and sister Juliana (five
  years younger)

planet than his pals. James, however, is not nearly
as indecisive and emotionally disorganized as
Dawson. Yes, he's sensitive and loyal and likable
and a dreamer, but he's also ambitious and determined and fully capable of charting his own path.
Pisces like being alone and getting lost; they dislike
being criticized and know-it-alls. Another famous
Pisces, Nirvana lead singer Kurt Cobain, shared
with James the sort of deep sensitivity, creative in-
tuitiveness, and soulful nature that is common to
Pisces.

And, like Cobain, who was taught to play guitar by an aunt, James can trace his many talents to
his family, specifically his loving parents. His athletic prowess, for instance, derives from his father,
Jim. Now an account executive with Southern New
England Telecommunications Corp., a cellular-
phone company, Jim once played professional
baseball for a minor-league club affiliated with the
Los Angeles Dodgers. Even though his father never
pressured him to follow in his footsteps, James
admits that his father's athleticism influenced him,
and that sports have always been a large part of his
life. Baseball, basketball, football, soccer—little
James tried them all, and he excelled at each and
every one. Even today, Beek is an exceptional athlete, reveling in physical pastimes like Jet Skiing
(he once told a reporter to climb aboard his Jet
Ski, and he then took her for a ten-minute thrill
ride that nearly knocked her off) and playing

pickup basketball (he's always on the prowl for a game in his downtime from filming *Dawson's*). Small wonder that, as shotgun-armed quarterback Jon Moxon in *Varsity Blues*, James was entirely convincing; he brought his own easy athleticism, honed by years of tossing the pigskin, to the role.

But don't go calling James a jock; he's much more complicated and multidimensional than that. There is, of course, his artistic side, which he owes to his mother, Melinda, a former Broadway dancer who now runs a gymnastics studio. When James was young, his mother ran a class for children, in which groups of kids would climb on a stage and perform gymnastics routines set to music. James remembers performing in one of his mother's recitals when he was a mere six years old, and credits his assurance in the world of theater, television, and movies to this early performing experience.

Young James was different in another way. When he was in kindergarten in Cheshire, he was diagnosed as having dyslexia, a learning disability that makes it difficult to read, and a disability that can, if undiagnosed and untreated, cause major problems later in life. Basically, people with dyslexia see certain letters reversed, leading to mispronunciations and acute frustration that uninformed observers may interpret as a lack of intelligence. Fortunately for James, his parents and teachers were aware of his dyslexia, and enrolled him in a special, experimental class, enabling him to learn to read on schedule. He went on to become a voracious reader, and today the shelves in his Wilmington apartment groan under the weight of books like James Joyce's *Portrait of the Artist As a Young Man*, J. D. Salinger's *Catcher in the Rye*, and other classics.

That's because James has another side besides jock and performer: he's also a secret intellectual. That's right, Beek the brawny football stud is just as at home in a library as he is on a playing field. "When I first met him, I was amazed at how smart and articulate he is," says his former *Dawson's* costar Mitchell Lawrence. "In fact, all of the actors were really smart kids. Joshua [Jackson] is an amazing guy, too, a very smart guy. I could sit with Josh and James and talk about all these things and they had this wealth of knowledge. And they have very strong opinions about things, too. James is very mature for his age and not afraid to tell you how he feels about stuff."

Growing up in Cheshire, James often went his own way, bucking the trends and bouncing to his own beat. He was quiet and introspective, sometimes appearing to others as if he were a million miles away. "I was in my own head, kind of a loner," he told *Interview* magazine. "To express how I was feeling I would write stories." One of his middle school English teachers encouraged James in his solitary pursuits, and made him feel it was okay not to follow the leader, that it was perfectly fine to strike out on his own. "He made me feel valuable for being different," James explained. It was such a powerful and important lesson that to this day James considers that middle school English teacher his mentor.

But James's quiet intelligence and inherent introversion had at least one undesirable consequence: growing up, he was not among the most popular kids in school. Hard to believe, but the boy who today can't go out without being mobbed by screaming female fans was considered, by his own recollection, a "dork" in school. "I never sat at the cool table," he recently said in an interview (wonder what those classmates who thought he was dorky think about him today?!). His TV character, Dawson Leery, is also shy and introspective—not unlike the actor who plays him. It's easy to understand how James can so convincingly inhabit the character of Dawson, how he can so seamlessly capture the fictional teen's sensitive and cerebral nature; all he has to do is reach inside himself and remember what he was like as a quiet young kid who didn't exactly fit in. One thing continues to baffle James, though. "I've often wondered why so many girls are attracted to Dawson," he told *TV Guide*, "because I was that big a dork in high school and nobody had a crush on me."

But there was one place that Beek did fit in, and that was the football field. Strapping on the shoulder pads, slipping on his helmet, he felt completely

Fish Story

James's Sign: Pisces, the Fish

Pisces' Birthstone: aquamarine

Pisces' Color of Choice: soft sea green

Pisces' Traits: imaginative, sensitive, compassionate

Pisces' Likes: solitude, mysteries, getting lost

Pisces' Dislikes: being criticized, know-it-alls

Ideal Date for Pisces: girls who are Cancers or Scorpios; girls who are warm, affectionate, sensitive, and like to cry in his element, able to do whatever he commanded his body to do. That is, until that fateful day when, jumping high to catch a pass, he came down with a concussion. He suffered no residual damage from the injury, but he definitely could not play any more tackle football that year. Suddenly he had all this extra time on his hands and nothing to do. He would need another activity to keep him occupied . . . what would it be?

The choice was easy; after all, it was in his blood. His concussion freed him up to do what he had first done at age six: perform. This time, however, he would try it in front of a larger audience than a bunch of proud parents. When a few of his friends decided to audition for a local community theater's production of *Grease*, James saw his chance and decided to audition, too.

It was his very first audition, and—big surprise—he nailed it.

James was cast as Danny Zuko, the lead character in *Grease*, a high-energy musical about a bunch of leather-jacket-wearing high schoolers in the 1950s. Danny (played by John Travolta in the movie version) was the coolest of the cool guys, caught between his greaser buddies and the love of a preppy girl at school. Who better to capture that youthful ambivalence than James, torn between his allegiance to his football pals and his secret interest in the arts? Once he got the part, however, James was hooked big time. He enjoyed everything about the theater—the rehearsals, the camaraderie, the chance to dye his blond hair black. "I just loved it," he later explained to one reporter. "I realized I was looking forward to every performance more than I was looking forward to Christmas." What's more, he told *Seventeen* magazine, "In *Grease* I got to be this cool guy who I never was in school." There was yet another benefit to becoming an actor: it was during *Grease* that James started dating his very first girlfriend. Everything about this "acting" thing seemed pretty great.

James Van Der Beek, actor, never looked back again.

His love affair with the theater continued when, after the eighth grade, James enrolled in the Cheshire Academy boarding school as a day student. Cheshire Academy, located on his hometown's main street, is a private, independent, coeducational school that has students in kindergarten all the way through the twelfth grade (and some postgraduate students as well). James was accepted on a full scholarship, and he did not disappoint the school's administrators. "During his four years at the academy he was a role model," a school spokesman told a reporter. Indeed, James was a town scholar, and regularly found himself on the honor roll. He also served as a student proctor, and was named a member of the National Honor Society (what a brain!).

Not surprisingly, James was something of a

favorite among the academy staff. At first, James dressed like every other boy at Cheshire—in the official uniform of jacket, tie, and suit pants. Eventually, though, he staged a mini-rebellion, and started showing up for classes in a pair of gray Dockers he loved instead of the suit pants. Even James was mildly surprised that not a single teacher or administrator ever said a word to him about the uniform violation. Other students got called in whenever they strayed from the official getup, but not James—*never* James. After all, he was the model student, and such a polite young man!

But all of his scholarly efforts and extracurricular activities took a toll on James's social life. "I never dated at all," he told *Seventeen* magazine. "I had like one friend." The truth is, James was much too busy immersing himself in the theater to worry about school dances and stuff like that. Once he made the decision to focus on acting, he demonstrated a resolve uncommon in someone his age. Yes, he kept playing sports and from time to time did all the other things that high school students do. But, inside, he was a changed person, and devoted most of his energy to learning his newfound craft. While other students were spending their time memorizing the lines to popular songs on the radio, James was holed up at the library, listening over and over again to a cast recording of the Broadway musical *Jesus Christ Superstar*. Other kids may have decorated their rooms with movie art (not unlike Dawson, who covers his walls with posters from *E.T.*, *Jaws*, and every movie ever made by his idol, Steven Spielberg), but James tacked up posters from *The Fantastiks* and other theatrical shows. Essentially, he had found something that moved and inspired him, that made him believe he belonged in this strange and exciting world. Singing along to the soundtrack of Broadway musicals, James was filled with confidence and determination. Performing was something he could do, something he was suited to even more than football—something that touched his heart and stirred his soul.

James had found his calling, and he was only fourteen years old.

For the next four years, James kept a foot in both camps, playing sports and pursuing acting. It wasn't always easy to juggle his twin passions. "The two worlds don't really coexist when you're fourteen or fifteen years old," James told *InStyle* magazine. "I would never pass out flyers to the guys on the team, like, 'Hey, guys, I'm doing *Godspell*. Check it out!'" As much as he may have wanted to run back from a good audition and tell his football pals about it, he never did. His theatrical aspirations just weren't something he could share with his sports buddies, so he largely kept them to himself, rehearsing for auditions in private at home and listening to his beloved musical cast albums in the sequestered safety of the library. Basically, James figured out that he had a different agenda than his fellow students, that he just couldn't be as carefree and happy-go-lucky as they were if he was to live his new dream and become an actor. So what if he couldn't share his passion with any classmate? He had something he loved doing, something no one could take away from him, something that made him feel mature and grown-up, and that was good enough.

It also really helped that James's parents were completely supportive of his acting ambitions. His mother, a seasoned performer, never tried to talk him out of it. In fact, James suspects that she had been secretly hoping that one of her children would follow in her footsteps and pursue a career in show business. Melinda could tell that her son James was dead serious about giving acting a shot, and what's more, that he had talent. As long as James maintained his studies, she would help him out. That meant accompanying him on the three-hour train ride into New York City, a place where he could audition not just for community theater productions like *Grease*, but for the real thing, the big time: Broadway! That took the kind of courage and determination that let his mother know her son wasn't merely indulging some passing fancy, that he wanted to be an actor more than he had ever wanted anything in his young life.

So Melinda Van Der Beek happily accompanied her son on his very first train ride into New York

City as an aspiring actor. They went straight to the office of a professional manager, the kind of busy place that's plastered with head shots and noisy with phones ringing off the hook. James dove into his audition and belted out a rendition of *Celebration*, a song from an old Tom Jones/Harvey Schmidt musical. He gave it everything he had, summoning up every bit of confidence he had built singing along to cast albums in the library back home. Sitting nearby, his mother Melinda was as surprised as anyone by the passion this youngster was demonstrating. She knew he was serious and talented, but it wasn't until that moment that she realized just how special her son might be. After the audition, James was quickly signed by an agent and a manager. A single trip to the city, and he already had a team of professionals in place to help launch his career. Young fifteen-year-old James Van Der Beek was on his way.

James would not, however, become an overnight success, despite this auspicious beginning. After he was signed, James had his acting head shot taken at a quickie photo place, posing in a variety of serious, actorly poses, trying his best to project the earnestness that he felt about his new craft. James and his mom would make the three-hour train ride into New York City and run around town, distributing his head shots to casting agents, because James believed that dropping off his head shots was a surefire strategy to quick recognition. He and his mother would make sandwiches before they set out into the city on the Metro North train line, and James remembers how they enjoyed their time together strolling the streets of New York, and how they liked to walk instead of taking taxi cabs. Unfortunately, James didn't book a single job for eighteen months. Taking the six-hour round-trip to New York City and coming home with nothing "was tough," James later recalled, "and could be very disheartening."

But he wasn't about to quit; not a chance of that. During the school year he would take an occasional trip to New York City after classes, but when the summer rolled around he went more frequently, usually around three times a week. After a while his mother stopped going with him, and James, still only fifteen, was venturing into the city by himself, going from audition to audition and trying not to feel dejected. His agents were sending him up for commercials, but he found that he was not particularly good at endorsing products. He would take it too seriously, and not deliver the clear message casting directors wanted. He tried not to think that it was something about his looks that kept him from getting hired for commercials, but to this day James marvels at the difficulty he's had booking commercial spots—in fact, he's appeared in only one, for a pimple treatment. Remember the teen who was happily "Oxy-cuting" his zits? That was James (ironically, when James filmed the commercial, his own skin was so broken out with acne, the producers had to use extra makeup to make him look clear-skinned).

Still it didn't bother James all that much that he wasn't getting commercials. Much as he would have liked to get work and draw a paycheck, his ultimate aspirations went far beyond pushing pimple cream. Right from the start, James was drawn to good material, to interesting projects, and his short résumé to date reflects an inquisitive mind determined to make adventurous career choices. With that kind of attitude, it isn't surprising at all that James's first big break involved one of America's most distinguished and unique playwrights, Edward Albee.

An enigmatic artist who saw popular success escape him for most his career, Albee was the daring dramatist behind *Who's Afraid of Virginia Woolf?*, a harsh, powerful play about a disintegrating marriage that would go on to become one of the classics of American theater (and later be made into a movie starring Elizabeth Taylor and Richard Burton). He was known for pioneering a stylized, highly ironic form of drama in plays like *The Zoo Story* and *A Delicate Balance*. The adopted son of millionaires who lived in Washington, D.C., Albee was an indifferent student who showed an aptitude for writing. And despite being thrown out of college in his sophomore year for not going to his prescribed classes (he was later also disowned by his parents), Albee went on to carve out one of the most singular careers in American theater, winning a prestigious Pulitzer Prize and a Tony Award along the way.

But despite his standing among the theatrical elite, Albee often saw his plays falter at the box office, and later in his career was happy to write and direct his own plays away from the Broadway spotlight, in smaller Off-Broadway theaters. *Finding the Sun*, about a young man who discovers some of life's secrets during a single day at the beach, was one such smaller-scale Albee effort.

Early one evening, James's agent called and asked him to go into New York City the next day to read for *Finding the Sun*. Perhaps fortunately, James wasn't all that up on his theatrical history, and didn't quite realize the exalted position Albee held among drama enthusiasts, although he knew that Albee was a theater professional of some stature and importance. Confident as ever, and only slightly nervous, James marched into the casting session and encountered Albee, all alone in the room.

The second major moment in James's life was about to happen.

James sat down, introduced himself, and went right into his monologue, the audition piece he had painstakingly prepared and honed over the weeks. In two minutes, it was over, and James got up to leave. There was no feedback, so James assumed he hadn't much impressed Albee—that his shot at getting the play was over. But before he walked out, he asked the playwright if there was any way he could improve his monologue. Albee replied that when he liked a bit of acting he didn't offer any suggestions about it.

It was all James needed to hear, and he practically floated out of the casting office. Edward Albee had told him he was good—no, better than good—and that was enough to *really* convince James that his dream of becoming an actor wasn't just a pipe dream. It didn't even matter if he got the part or not—in fact, he had a pretty good idea that he hadn't. More important, he'd received a pat on the back from Edward Albee, a boost that completely reenergized his grinding pursuit of his dream.

Naturally, he got the part. It was his first major theatrical audition and—as James had at other key moments in his life and would again in the future—he nailed it.

Looking back, James figures that Albee liked his honesty and lack of attitude. He was young and he was adventurous, willing to try anything and not be hung up on any methods or techniques. In essence, he was a blank slate—something he guesses was immensely appealing to Albee the director. But there's another reason why Albee was likely drawn to James. As a teenager, Albee attended the Choate

School in Connecticut, a tony learning institution that was in many ways similar to the Cheshire Academy. So when Albee went looking for someone to play the part of Fergus—described in the playbill as "sixteen; blond, handsome, healthy kid; swimmer's body"—he knew exactly the kind of fresh-scrubbed kid he was searching for, someone with the kind of preppy, New Englandish radiance he had encountered while at Choate. Needless to say, James fit the bill.

Once he got the part of Fergus, James maintained the earnestness and malleability (typical Pisces traits) he had demonstrated at the audition, rather than letting his success go to his head. He approached rehearsals with unbridled enthusiasm and a total openness to instruction; it was, for James, the best acting school he could have hoped for. And the lessons he learned would come in handy further down the road. From Albee, James later told a reporter, "I learned what it meant to be good, how to reach down inside myself."

It was the first example of what would become a Van Der Beek trait: an eagerness to learn, to always improve himself, to see himself as a student at the hands of more experienced artists, rather than as some kind of star. "He's a very humble guy," says Patrick Read Johnson, his director on *Angus*. "At the audition for the movie, I could tell right away how serious he was, how much more mature than the other young actors he was. He really listened when I gave him directions. He didn't just nod his head and say, 'Okay, sure.' He asked questions and he really wanted to know what I wanted. And that continued during the shoot as well. He was really keen on learning."

Mark Tarlov, a veteran movie producer who worked with James on a 1997 film called *I Love You, I Love You Not*, saw the same thing. "You can always tell what kind of an actor you have by the questions they ask," says Tarlov. "I did a movie with Holly Hunter and Sigourney Weaver called *Copycat*, and it was just stunning to see the kinds of questions these actresses were asking about what they were doing. They were just so perceptive and so far beyond the normal level of questions like, 'Should I pick that up now?' And that's what James's questions about the material were like. That's the kind of thing he had going. And that, I think, is how you can tell if an actor is the real deal. James is."

Even when he got the call for *Dawson's Creek*, a gig that could have swelled any young actor's head, James approached the job as another opportunity to learn from his more experienced costars and improve his acting skills. "He was a very hard worker," says his former *Creek* costar Mitchell Lawrence. "All of them—James, Josh, Katie, Michelle—were really hard workers. With James, he was always completely professional, always willing to experiment a little bit, to push himself."

Perhaps James realized early on that he would have to stay completely focused to gain an edge over all the other talented young actors out there competing for the same jobs. For instance, he later learned that the mesmerizing actor Ed Norton, nominated for an Oscar for *American History X*, had also auditioned for the lead role in Edward Albee's *Finding the Sun*. Norton later told James that he desperately wanted the part that James had won. But Norton, who became friends with James, would have his sweet revenge. When the juicy role of a young sociopath opened up in the Richard Gere courtroom thriller *Primal Fear* in 1996, both James and Ed Norton wanted the part so badly they would have cut off a pinkie to get it. The role went to Norton and turned him into a major star.

James's big break would arrive soon enough. For the moment, he was happy to be acting in an Edward Albee play, not at the local YMCA but in New York City, the center of the theater world. His role as Fergus in *Finding the Sun* included one big monologue, in Scene 13. Delivered directly to the audience, it was a particularly challenging demand on any actor. With the stage dimmed and empty of any other actors and the spotlight squarely on his shoulders, James approached the audience every night and totally mesmerized them with his youthful, accessible charm. "If you think it's easy being my age, well . . . you have another thing coming," he began. "A New England boyhood isn't all peaches and cream, maple syrup and russet autumns. I know it sounds pretty good—wealthy mother and all, private school . . . I'm not complaining, it's nice. But it isn't always nice." James was completely believable in his portrayal of an outwardly carefree but inwardly tormented teenager—just as he would be later on playing a similar character, Dawson Leery.

James finished the Albee play and soon landed another meaty part, in a production of the musical *Shenandoah* at the Goodspeed Opera House in New York City. Strangely, he was one of four actors named James on the production, which gave birth to his other nickname—Baby James (he was the youngest of the four, and his castmates were big fans of the James Taylor song "Sweet Baby James"). Once again James looked at the job as a chance to flex his acting muscles, to learn and grow and improve his burgeoning skills. "The minute you stop learning," James told *E! Online*, "it's time to quit."

But quitting was not something that James had any intention of doing. In his senior year at the Cheshire Academy, he felt the urge to broaden his horizons, to push his career in a new direction. He had tried musical theater and done really well. Plus he was getting a little tired of schlepping into New York City for commercial auditions that weren't going anywhere. It was time, he figured, to pursue his ultimate goal: film work.

It was time for James Van Der Beek to make his move. And make it he did—big time.

CHAPTER TWO

Angus Away!

To get from the leafy comfort of Cheshire, Connecticut, all the way to the gritty streets of Hollywood, California, you have to travel some 2,500 miles, or roughly five hours by plane. But to James Van Der Beek, the journey was more than geographic. It was a quantum leap from the sheltered safety of his hometown, and the protective familiarity of the theater world, to a strange and unwelcoming land where his wildest dreams could come true—or, just as easily, be crushed.

James, as usual, was up for the challenge. He was a bright man with a big goal—to act in movies—and he approached it with the same fierce determination that had turned him into an accomplished stage presence after only a few plays. Sure, he was just sixteen years old, and, sure, Hollywood routinely shatters the spirit of much older movie wannabes, but James wasn't your average aspiring actor; he had already proved that by nailing his very first major theater audition. He was also a serious student of the cinema; much like Dawson Leery, the character he would soon bring to life, James admired and studied the movies of Francis Ford Coppola, Martin Scorsese, Oliver Stone, and, yes, Steven Spielberg. Call it youthful bravado or call it a preternatural poise, but James simply felt that if he was going to make the switch from watching movies to making them, he might as well get started.

His parents were right where they had been all along—solidly behind their son. In the summer of 1995, following his junior year at Cheshire Academy, James told his folks about his desire to give Hollywood a go. They agreed to accompany him to California, where he would make the rounds, turn up at a few auditions, and more or less get his feet wet in the film biz. Then, if nothing panned out, it would be back to school for his senior year. That summer the Van Der Beek clan of Cheshire, Connecticut, decamped to sunny Los Angeles.

Waiting for him there was a hungry young director in the market for fresh, compelling talent. Patrick Read Johnson, a bright and amiable Irishman, had been dubbed Hollywood's Flavor of the Month by *Premiere* magazine after his first movie—a clever, low-budget, independently made science-fiction comedy called *Spaced Invaders*— caught the eye of Steven Spielberg and turned Johnson into a hot commodity. *Spaced Invaders*,

Famous Firsts

First time onstage: in a gymnastics
  show, at age six
First theater role: Danny Zuko in
  Grease
First TV role: a guest shot on *Clarissa
  Explains It All*, 1991
First movie role: Rick Sandford in
  Angus
First onscreen kiss: with Ariana
  Richards in *Angus*
First movie he ever saw: *E.T.*
First concert he ever attended: Green
  Day
First talk show he was on: *The
  Tonight Show* with Jay Leno
Age when he had his first girlfriend:
  thirteen
Age when he bought his first
  computer: twenty-one

made on a shoestring for about $2 million, told the story of a band of goofy Martians who descend on a small Illinois town, having mistaken Orson Welles's infamous 1938 radio parody of an alien invasion for legitimate marching orders. Spielberg was particularly taken with one of the actresses in *Spaced Invaders*: Ariana Richards. "Where did you find her?" he asked Johnson. "She's terrific." Spielberg would go on to cast Richards as Lex Murphy, the young female lead fleeing mutant dinosaurs in his megablockbuster *Jurassic Park*.

Spielberg liked *Spaced Invaders* enough to suggest to Disney Pictures that they pick it up and release it, which they did. Critics weren't crazy about the film, but it made a decent profit, and Johnson parlayed it into a movie deal with Universal Studios. He had also been courted by Disney Pictures, but was informed by then-Disney executive Jeffrey Katzenberg that if he signed with the studio, he would be asked to cut his teeth by making short films for Disney's theme-park rides. Having already directed a feature-length film, Johnson didn't like the idea very much, and opted instead for the Universal deal, which, among other things, afforded him his own bungalow on the Universal lot.

Johnson made a movie for producer John Hughes (of *The Breakfast Club* fame) called *Baby's Day Out*—a sweet and funny film that had the great misfortune to open on the same weekend as

The Lion King, all but eliminating any chance it had to turn a profit. Then Johnson turned his attention to a script called *Angus*, a small and tender story about an overweight teenager, Angus Bethune, who is constantly tormented by his classmates. In the original version of the movie, Angus not only had to defend himself against his fellow students because he was fat, but also because his father was gay—a story twist that made Angus's travails all that much more poignant. But when that version of the movie was screened for a young audience, they reacted negatively to the idea that Angus's father was gay. "The day after the screening, we got a note from the studio: 'Lose the gay father,'" Johnson sadly recalls. "The movie got heavily cut and, I think, suffered for it."

Before filming, though, Johnson was bursting with optimism about the project. He really loved the story: set in a typical midwestern high school, it revolves around a smart but chubby student who is elected King of the Prom—a practical joke played by his classmates—and must decide whether to attend the prom. If he goes, he knows he will be the object of some cruel prank. But if he doesn't go, he'll never get the chance to dance with Melissa, the beautiful, fair-haired girl who was elected prom queen, and with whom he has been secretly in love since grade school. Angus's rival for Melissa's affections is Rick, the school's quarterback and the town's most popular teen, a guy who has managed to get the best of Angus ever since they were little kids. To Johnson, it looked like the sweet and classic tale of a misfit who follows his heart and triumphs over adversity. He set the movie up with New Line Cinema and Turner Pictures, and got right down to the business of casting.

Identifying and hiring great actors is clearly one of Johnson's strengths. He knew he wanted to work with Ariana Richards again, so he sent her the script and asked her to play Melissa. Fresh from her role in *Jurassic Park*, one of the biggest-grossing movies of all time, she told Johnson she loved the script and signed on for the movie. Johnson also got Oscar-winning actress Kathy Bates, who had been so scarily convincing in *Misery*, to play Angus's mother, and even signed legendary actor George C. Scott to play Angus's grandfather. Still to be cast were the key roles of Angus and his rival Rick.

For Angus, Johnson wanted someone new and fresh, someone who could easily inhabit his complex and touching leading character. He auditioned hundreds of young actors, but never found anyone who projected the kind of sincerity he was looking for. After one particularly frustrating New York casting session, Johnson hopped in his car and headed for his hometown, Chicago. Along the way, he got thirsty, and pulled over into a Wendy's in Lake Forest, Illinois. "I'm standing in line, and I hear all these girls giggling and laughing behind the cash registers, and they're laughing and saying, 'Oh, Charlie, you're so funny!' And I look to see who they're talking about and I see this chubby kid, Charlie Talbert, cracking jokes. And then I get this big director's grin on my face." Johnson had just seen Angus!

He got to the front of the line, ordered his drink, and dropped a bombshell on Charlie Talbert. "Hey, do you want to be in a movie?" he asked. Charlie explained that he had no background in acting at all, except for an appearance in a fourth-grade production of *Romeo and Juliet*. Johnson handed him his business card and, the next day, Charlie went to a casting office and auditioned for the role of Angus. "The casting director called me and said, 'You've got to see this kid,'" Johnson recalls. "Turns out he's a complete and utter natural." And that's how an overweight Wendy's cashier with zero acting experience landed the lead role in a major motion picture.

Not yet cast, though, was the pivotal role of Rick Sandford, Angus's childhood rival and the closest thing to a villain in the movie. Rick is the football-team captain, the town's golden boy, an all-American dream teen with a nasty streak in his personality. "The kind of guy," James later told *Teen People*, "who would have beat up Dawson." Rick is the one who gives Angus the most grief about his weight, and about his affections for Melissa. For the role, Johnson wanted someone who could capture the character's outward appeal, but also project his anger and pain. It was a small but terribly important part, and he needed an actor who could make Rick seem frightening without being totally villainous; an actor who could turn him into the complex and multidimensional character he would need to be to make the movie succeed. "I wanted Rick to be charming and good-looking," says Johnson, "but I also wanted him to have a dark side."

In the summer of 1994, Johnson set up numerous casting sessions in New York and Los Angeles. They were open casting calls, the kind of brutal experiences where actors are herded into the room in groups and dispatched after brief auditions. The starting shoot date for *Angus* was quickly approaching, so when Johnson set up a casting call in a building on Olympic Boulevard in Los Angeles, he felt a real urgency to find the right actor to play Rick. "We were seeing a lot of actors, ten of them an hour," he says. "You know, come in, read for a couple of minutes, thank you very much, see you later." It was getting late in the day and no one was blowing Johnson's socks off; he was sure he'd have to wrap up another casting session without finding his Rick.

"And then," Johnson recalls, "in walked James."

Walking into that office on Olympic Boulevard was the third major moment in James's life.

There was no clap of thunder, no bolt of lightning to herald the arrival of Hollywood's next great actor. But there were definitely signs that something special was happening. "It was just one of those remarkable things," says Johnson, who was in the room with studio head Dawn Steel, a female casting director, and several other women. "I looked around the room and I watched the women watch James, and I said, 'Okay, I can practically see their pupils dilating and the hairs standing up on their arms.' There was a very visible reaction to this guy entering the room, a kind of animal electricity coming off him."

James hadn't even said a word, and already he had everyone riveted. For one thing, his appearance set him apart from the hundreds of hopefuls who had preceded him. "Most of the guys had long hair, unlaced boots, a lot of attitude, sort of surly," says Johnson. "James was smart, he played it differently. He was clean cut, and he dressed like a normal guy. I knew the minute I saw him that he wasn't from New York or Los Angeles, and that meant a lot. He also looked like an all-American, the kind of guy that all the girls in high school would just say, 'Wow, he's the best!'" Little did Johnson know that, in reality, James was hardly the golden boy at Cheshire Academy, and that he actually thought of himself as a dork.

In that casting office, though, James was transformed. He was in his element now, and his confidence and intelligence shone through. "He didn't have to put anything out," says Johnson. "He did the opposite. He played it straight and had no pretension at all. He was simply there to meet, shake hands, be as pleasant as possible, and read the lines." Future directors and producers would be just as impressed by James's rare ability to convey his smarts and sincerity with the simplest of gestures. "He is wonderfully understated," says Mark Tarlov, his producer on *I Love You, I Love You Not.* "He allows you to feel what he wants you to feel, rather than coming right at you and screaming in your face. And he does it without yelling or hitting all the obvious marks. That's one of the reasons kids like him—they don't like it when actors are stupid and do the obvious things, and they can figure out what someone is going to say five minutes before they say it. James's style is to make his point in a way that seems organic to what he's doing."

James's charisma was so overwhelming that, before he even said a word to Johnson, his fate had been decided. "I knew right away, before he even read for us, that James was going to play the part of Rick," declares Johnson. "I said to myself, 'I'm casting this guy, he's *it*.' Because I really felt this energy, this kind of young Tom Cruise thing. There's absolutely nothing phony about him."

James's chances of playing the part only improved once he introduced himself to everyone and began reading scenes from the script. "He had this great voice, this non–New York and non–L.A. voice," says Johnson. "It was the perfect middle-American voice." Not surprisingly, James was allowed to audition for a much longer block of time than any actor who had come in that day. It wasn't that Johnson needed him to read line after line after line: he knew within a minute of meeting James that he wanted him for the role. But Johnson wanted to test him, to determine what his acting range was, and to see how well he took direction. Once again, he was quickly impressed.

When James finished reading and walked out of the room, Johnson turned to studio head Dawn Steel and announced, "That's him, that's Rick." Steel took a more cautious approach, but admitted that James had indeed been the best of the bunch so far. Johnson had taped James's audition, and the next day sent the videotape around. "Everyone agreed that, by far, James stood out from the pack," says Johnson. "He was completely untrained, and he was completely unaware of what he has, but nevertheless he just stood out." Studio heads, film producers, friends, and family members all got a look at the tape, as opinions were solicited about this exciting young actor Johnson was determined to cast in his movie. Everyone agreed: James was a special talent. Johnson spent a few more days auditioning actors for Rick, but in his heart the part had already been cast.

It was one of his very first auditions for a major motion picture, and—big surprise—Beek nailed it.

A casting director called James to give him the good news. *Angus* would start filming in September, and stretch on for eight weeks. That meant that James would have to take a semester off from the Cheshire Academy, and that he would have to make that semester up on his own—in essence, completing two semesters at once—if he was to graduate on time. No problem. James wound up missing a month and a half of his senior year so that he could make his motion picture debut in *Angus*.

James arrived for his first wardrobe session "all smiles," says Johnson. "He was really delighted and sort of blushing and kind of kicking the dirt—very humble." Soon it was off to Owatonna, Minnesota, a small town selected by Johnson because it struck him as typically quaint and midwestern. The cast and crew were put up at the Owatonna Ramada Inn, a modest little hotel that—to all the giddy and inexperienced youngsters in the movie—must have seemed like their own private fun house. James's parents accompanied him to Minnesota for part of the shoot (his father even had a small, nonspeaking role in one scene, playing Rick's father sitting in the stands during a football game). But for the rest of it James was alone—away from home and on his own for the first time. It's a testament to his character and upbringing that James—and, indeed, all of the other young actors—behaved appropriately and maturely throughout the entire shoot. "They had curfews and they had guardians," says Johnson. "We tried to make sure they were all in bed by a certain time. But there's no way to make sure they go to sleep at the right time." Still, James never showed up for work late, never showed any signs that he had partied through the night, and always appeared alert and well rested. He was a model of professionalism in his very first professional film job.

The cast of *Angus* had exactly one week to rehearse. That was more than enough time for Johnson, who didn't like to overrehearse young actors. It had been his experience that the more they went over their lines, the more mannered and self-conscious their performances would become. Sometimes the very first line delivery was the best. And, Johnson knew, younger actors tend to get bored quicker. Even the superb cast he had assembled for *Angus* had its moments of immaturity, when the youngsters would get tired and silly and become incapable of focusing on the work. At those times, Johnson came to depend on one of his actors—James Van Der Beek. "Sometimes, you could see this impatience in his face, this darkness, and you could feel him getting serious and wanting the others to get serious, too," the director recalls. "At the end of long days when some of the actors would get punch-drunk and goofy and start cracking up, James was always the one who said, 'Hey, come on, it's time to do the work.' He has incredible focus."

It was not surprising that James was able to establish himself as a leader among his peers. He had been trained in the theater, where discipline and concentration were essential attributes. On top of that, James has a natural leadership quality—not because he dominates every situation he's in, but because he doesn't. "He's not a loud person at all," Johnson observes. "He lets other people make a lot of noise, and then he steps in with something clever. He bides his time and waits for his moment, and he draws people to him this way."

The young actors formed cliques, just as teenagers do in high school. Early on, James became the leader of his clique. He hung around mainly with the actors who were playing his two buddies in the movie, Salim Grant and Kevin Connolly. They became a sort of "junior Rat Pack," Johnson says with a laugh. "They were the bad guys in the movie, and they had all the girls chasing them on the set." Likewise, young Charlie Talbert, cast as Angus, hung around with his sidekick in the movie, Chris Owen. Perhaps inevitably, Charlie and Chris never got too friendly with James and his pals, who played their rivals in the film.

The shoot itself went splendidly, with no controversy and minimal disruptions. They spent five weeks in Owatonna, and three more shooting interior scenes in Los Angeles. Johnson remembers the first scene he shot with James—the very first moment when James acted in front of a movie camera. "The shot is supposed to be from Angus's point of view," he says. "We're seeing Angus watch James and Ariana, who plays Angus's object of affection, sit at a picnic table and have lunch with their friends. We can't hear what they're saying, but we can see this cluster of friends that Angus isn't a part of." Interestingly, James's first chance to shine would come in a scene without any dialogue. In fact, he was fifty feet away from the camera, sitting among a group of other actors—a tough position from which to distinguish yourself. But the scene required James's character Rick to turn toward the camera and stare menacingly at Angus, and that's just what James did—superbly. "He just shot over this really riveting, awful, evil look," Johnson remembers. "I was looking at him on the monitor, and, right away, he was able to turn it on. I just said, 'Wow, this guy has presence.'"

The key to that charisma, says Johnson, is in James's eyes. "He has this really amazing control over his eyes, an amazing range of things he can do with his eyes. In many ways, his good looks and his strong jaw and his smile and his hair sometimes get in the way of his eyes, which are so expressive on film. The more you can get in on his eyes, the more you'll get out of him as an actor. He really knows how to let his eyes do the work and tell the story."

Many of James's remaining scenes were on the football field. Johnson had cast James without knowing that he had a background in football, or that he had once harbored aspirations of playing professionally. But it soon became apparent that James was a skilled athlete, and that Johnson would not have to intercut scenes of someone else throwing a football—James was perfectly convincing as the high school's top jock. "Once we got him into the pads and the helmet, he really looked terrific on film," says Johnson. "He could throw, he could run, he looked like an athlete—he was just perfect."

One scene required James's character to terrorize Angus, to show his true colors and turn really mean. Johnson was amazed at the depth of hatred James was able to convey. "The anger that came out really surprised me," he says. "It made me realize that he can really go there, that he has a dark side he has access to." Another scene, the big prom scene, required James to turn on the charm and act the part of the classic leading man. No problem at all for Beek. Some 4,500 extras jammed into a gymnasium in Los Angeles, playing high schoolers at the prom. "The girls are all just staring at James, just trying to get a good look at him," Johnson says. "They're definitely buzzing about James. And the guys are checking James out, too, because he's the cool guy." Once again, Johnson realized what he had on his hands—a remarkable actor who was also a charismatic star.

As rare as that combination is, it's even rarer to find such an actor who is also consistently professional. And yet here was James, still a teenager and in his first movie, acting like the consummate pro. "I never, ever had to worry about James during the making of this film," says Johnson. "I knew he would always be able to handle himself. And he didn't go around asking for extra lines to fill out his part or make it more this or that. What he did instead was humanize the character quietly, in his own way. A lot of the extra touches he gave the material were eventually cut from the movie, but he certainly gave me enough to make for a deeper character. A lot of other young actors would have played Rick as just a nasty guy, but James invested him with a degree of complexity that the part didn't even have." Johnson wasn't the only one raving about James's performance. "Everyone who came in and watched the dailies with us said, 'This guy is going to be a big star,'" Johnson says. "All my friends, everyone's friends, they all said, 'Gee, this guy is . . . wow!'"

The film wrapped in the late fall of 1994, and James soon returned to Connecticut. For Johnson, however, the real drama was just beginning. After early test screenings scared studio executives into eliminating the gay-father angle, Johnson essentially lost control of the movie. He went on a much-needed vacation with his wife while Dawn Steel reedited the movie. Months later, Johnson nervously attended a screening of the new version of *Angus*, the project he had nurtured and lovingly created. To his total surprise, the movie had been changed from a sweet, tender coming-of-age story into a loud and messy teen comedy. A song by Green Day was added to jazz things up, and whole scenes were recut to give them an edgy, choppy MTV-style look. Johnson was devastated, and quickly realized that the movie would not be commercially successful.

Indeed, it wasn't. James was enrolled as a freshman at Drew University when, in 1995, *Angus* was released in theaters. He remembered people telling him on the set that the movie was going to make him a huge star, and so he was looking forward to the movie's premiere with plenty of anticipation. He had only been at Drew for two weeks, but he had already made some good friends, and he rounded them up to go with him to see *Angus* the day it opened. There was only one problem: neither James nor any of his buddies had a car. He wanted to see the eight P.M. screening, and here it was, ten minutes before showtime and no set of wheels in sight. James was also upset because an old girlfriend had promised to drop by campus that night and see him, but she blew him off. The young actor who many had predicted would soon be a major star didn't have a date and couldn't get a ride to his own movie. Some big shot he was.

James finally did get a ride to the theater and saw himself on the big screen for the first time. He was disappointed, and he wasn't the only one. The reviews weren't terrible—more like lukewarm. "A formulaic teen-inspiration tale that manages to raise itself slightly above the average for teen-oriented flicks," wrote Gary Kamiya of the *San Francisco Examiner*. "It's hard to argue with the sentiments expressed, but there are definitely some missing moves here." Susan Wloszczyna of *USA Today* called it "well-meaning," with an "overly familiar script that could have used more meat on its own bones." Johnson read the reviews and wanted to scream. "It was frustrating," he says now. "All of the things they said were wrong with the movie were the things I knew were wrong, too. They didn't get to see the movie I wanted to make."

Only Roger Ebert, the well-known critic from the *Chicago Sun-Times*, gushed about *Angus*. On the portly side himself, Ebert clearly identified with the movie's overweight hero. "Here it is at last," he wrote, "after years and years and years: A movie where the smart fat kid gets the girl and humiliates the football hero." Angus's triumph at the end of the film moved Ebert to compare it to another underdog movie. Angus, he wrote, "scores a victory for fat kids everywhere in a climax that I, for one, found wholly the equal of anything in *Rocky*."

But despite predictions that the film would make a star out of James Van Der Beek, *Angus* came and went without a splash. Very few reviews singled out James, most likely because his role had been cut and he wound up seeming "basically like a one-note character," Johnson says. Stardom would have to wait for James; suddenly he was just another struggling actor bouncing from audition to audition. For the first time in a while, doubts crept into James's mind. Maybe he wasn't destined to become the great actor he thought he could be. Maybe it really was just a pipe dream.

But Patrick Read Johnson knew differently. Never mind that the critics didn't single James out—after all, the entire movie was pretty much destroyed in the editing process. A truer measure of James's potential, he thought, could be found in the scores from the test screenings of Johnson's original version of the movie. "The rest of the characters received pretty much what you would expect," Johnson recalls. "But James's numbers were through the roof. I mean, his numbers were really staggering!"

The man who discovered James Van Der Beek knew something few other people knew: the career of a truly great actor had just been launched. "I knew that he had staying power," says Patrick

Read Johnson. "I knew that he was definitely going to make it."

James would not have to wait very long to get another shot at movie stardom.

CHAPTER THREE

In *Love* with Movies

Billy Hopkins knew a thing or two about James Van Der Beek. One of the best and busiest casting directors on the East Coast, Hopkins had auditioned James for several movie parts, and had always been impressed by his skill and likability. He was also familiar with James's theater work, and knew the young actor had the range to play a wide variety of parts. On top of that, a friend of his, Anne Thompson, had had a small part in the movie *Angus*, and couldn't say enough nice things about her costar, James. "She would tell me how wonderful he was," says Hopkins. "So we knew about James when it came time to cast the movie."

The movie was something called *I Love You, I Love You Not*. It was based on a one-act play that Hopkins had directed at New York City's Ensemble Studio Theater way back in 1983, and now it had been blown into a full-length screenplay by Hopkins's friend Wendy Kesselman. Hopkins liked the script so much, he decided to make *I Love*

You, I Love You Not his very first project as a director.

Hopkins had broken into the business as a casting director on Madonna's 1985 movie debut, *Desperately Seeking Susan*. After that, Hopkins hardly ever came up for air, working on several movies each year and helping cast such hit films as *Wall Street*, with Charlie Sheen; *True Romance*, with Christian Slater; *Seven*, with Brad Pitt; *The Rock*, with Nicolas Cage; and *Good Will Hunting*, starring Matt Damon. He developed a reputation as an astute evaluator of young talent, someone who could cast a small but important role with just the right unknown face to make it work. He'd also directed a number of plays in New York City, and had come to a true and deep understanding of good actors and good acting.

When the screenplay for *I Love You, I Love You Not* landed on his desk in 1993, it came with a suggestion from the writer Wendy Kesselman that Hopkins himself direct the script. Hopkins found the suggestion odd, since he was in the middle of a nasty, five-year feud with Kesselman, who had been a very close friend. He was surprised that she would recommend him for the movie, but through her agent she passed along her belief that he was the perfect man for the job. "She said, 'You've directed theater for so long, and we know that at some point you're going to direct a movie, and I think you'd be right for this,'" Hopkins recalls.

Acting Up

Actors James has been compared to: Tom Cruise, James Stewart, Ethan Hawke

Great actors he's worked with: George C. Scott, Kathy Bates, Jeanne Moreau, Claire Danes, Jon Voight

Great actor he'd most like to work with: Paul Newman

Actor friends: Edward Norton, Joshua Jackson

Most common praise for his acting: self-assured, likeable, intense

Best feature as an actor: his eyes

His advice to actors: never stop learning

His advice to would-be actors: find another line of work

Greatest acting challenge on *Dawson's*: staying clean-shaven!

The two friends buried the hatchet and decided to make *I Love You, I Love You Not* as soon as possible.

The movie tells the story of Daisy, a young Jewish girl at a stuffy private high school who discovers that her grandmother survived the Holocaust. As the pretty but awkward Daisy coaxes her "Nana" to tell her more and more about her time at the Auschwitz concentration camp, she also takes an interest in Ethan, the school's handsome golden boy. Daisy's fascination with the horrors of the Holocaust coincides with her own first brush with racism at the hands of Ethan and his preppy classmates, who ostracize Daisy because she is Jewish (the title refers to Daisy's ruminations on whether Ethan really loves her). "I knew right away that it wouldn't be a commercial movie, that it would be very difficult to market," admits Hopkins. "So I said to myself, 'We just have to go get some really great actors.'"

Hopkins teamed up with his friend and frequent movie partner Mark Tarlov, a veteran producer with movies like *Copycat*, *Serial Mom*, and *Christine* on his résumé. Tarlov liked the script and liked the idea of Hopkins directing, but he also realized that they would need a stellar cast to help sell the film. It was going to take all of Hopkins's many skills as a casting director to round up the right group of actors to bring this small, subtle story to life. The first role that Hopkins thought about filling was the crucial part of the grandmother, Nana. He needed a European actress with enough presence to compensate for what would otherwise be a very youthful and inexperienced cast. Hopkins set his sights high: he wanted veteran French actress Jeanne Moreau, best known for starring in the François Truffaut classic *Jules and Jim*. Moreau's representatives told Hopkins she wasn't available, but Hopkins knew that she was going to be in New York City for a retrospective of her movies, and he sent his movie script to her hotel. "She called me and told me she liked the script very much, and she would love to have me come to Paris and meet with her and talk about it," Hopkins says. "I went to Paris with Mark and Wendy, and Jeanne agreed to do it."

With a well-known European actress in place as the anchor of the cast, Hopkins turned his attention to the lead role of Daisy. As it turned out, Mark Tarlov's business partner is married to the actress Bess Armstrong, who had been in the critically acclaimed, teen-oriented TV series *My So-Called Life*, which starred Claire Danes as the angst-filled Angela. Danes was also the female lead in the hit film *Romeo and Juliet*, opposite Leonardo DiCaprio, and looked like she was on her way to major movie stardom. Tarlov got her the script for *I Love You, I Love You Not*, and she, too, agreed to come aboard. The pieces were starting to fall into place for Hopkins and crew.

The next crucial role to be filled was Ethan, the handsome, popular student who breaks Daisy's heart. Hopkins auditioned a number of people, and actually cast one young actor in the part. But that actor, Hopkins noticed, was unable to keep up with Danes, a remarkable and powerful actress with extensive theatrical training. Hopkins and Tarlov next settled on a young British actor named Jude Law, who at the time was making a huge splash on Broadway in a play called *Indiscretions*. But it wasn't just Law's acting that had critics and audiences buzzing, it was the scene in which he appeared onstage completely nude. Miramax, the studio which had agreed to back the movie, was keen on casting Law, who to that point had only appeared in one full-length movie, 1994's *Shopping*. Hopkins and Tarlov agreed: Law would be their Ethan.

Only one major role remained to be cast: the part of Tony, Ethan's best friend. "He's the second in command of the big clique at school, right behind Ethan," says Tarlov. "He's a very privileged kid and he's very harsh on Daisy, very judgmental, because she's different. He sort of looks down his nose at this little Jewish girl who likes his best friend." It was the closest thing to a villain in the movie, and it required an actor who could bring power and subtlety to the role. Years earlier, Hopkins had attended a prep school in Buffalo, New York, and so he knew the character of Tony inside and out—a snooty, self-infatuated blue blood in a blazer. "Basically, I was looking for my friends in eighth grade," he says. One name popped right into Hopkins's mind: James Van Der Beek. "He was submitted by his agent for the part," says Hopkins, "but he was on my list of actors to bring in, too."

It was the summer of 1995, and James was just finishing up his senior year at Cheshire Academy. The year before he had filmed *Angus*, and he was more than ready for another crack at the movies. He took the train into New York City and auditioned for the part of Tony, not knowing that Hopkins had him in mind for the role. "At the first audition, James was just great," Hopkins recalls. "He was brilliant! I said to Wendy, 'My gosh, this guy is going to be a big movie star.' The thing is, he was auditioning for this Waspy, blue-blooded boy and he himself did not come from that kind of family. His family is a very middle-of-the-road, working-class family with an artistic side. But James can play both sides. He can play upper class and lower class just as convincingly, which a lot of actors can't do."

Mark Tarlov saw a videotape of James's audition and was just as taken with the young actor. "He was without question the best of the group we brought in," says Tarlov. As usual, James was able to make an impression without even opening his mouth. "He walks in and he just has this presence," says Hopkins. "Not in any off-putting way; it's just there. When you meet him he's this nice, regular guy, and then he reads for this part of a mean kid, and he was just . . . no one had read the part like that! Wendy, the writer, just got chills." What set James apart from other young actors was his "total lack of pretense," says Hopkins. "A lot of guys come in and they're doing all that mumbly James Dean stuff, none of which James was doing."

James was so good in his first audition for the part of Tony that Hopkins and Kesselman started thinking he might be able to handle the lead role of Ethan. "We talked about how he could do it, if we didn't already have an actor," says Hopkins. "But he was also so good in the part of Tony that I thought, 'If I do move him, who am I going to get to do this part who's as good as he is?'" The director saw a few other actors for the part of Tony, but he had already made up his mind: James was a star in the making, and he wanted him in his movie.

Actually, James came closer to getting the role of Ethan in *I Love You, I Love You Not* than he ever realized. Jude Law, then appearing in *Indiscretions* with Kathleen Turner, had been granted a work visa to enter the United States just for the duration of the play. Tarlov worked feverishly to get Law a second visa for the movie, but it was slow going—so slow that the production was actually in its second day of filming when Law's second visa finally came through. "James was Plan B," says Tarlov. "He was very close to being promoted to the lead. And he could have done it. He did not look like an actor who had only done one movie." Hopkins, too, says he would have been perfectly comfortable shifting James into the top spot. "I wouldn't have had to reaudition him or anything," he says. "I would have just said, 'James, you're playing Ethan now.'"

That Hopkins and Tarlov were willing to entrust so much of their $2.5 million movie to an eighteen-year-old actor who had only played a small role in one previous film speaks highly of the impression he made on the filmmakers. "He's like a breath of fresh air when he walks into a room," Hopkins notes. "There's an intensity to him, but it doesn't come out when you first meet him. He's just a sweet, regular guy. But when he puts his mind to the work, he's very serious and focused. He was a consummate professional right out of the chute."

But the consummate professional had one little problem: the start of shooting coincided with his senior prom. Hopkins did the honorable thing and delayed James's start date so he could attend his graduation and his prom. After that, James dedicated himself 100 percent to *I Love You, I Love*

You Not. "He was thrilled to get the part," says Hopkins. "It was the summer, it was his second movie, and he got along with all the other young actors. We all had a lot of fun making the movie."

Much of the film would be shot at the New York Jewish Theological Seminary, an old building on Manhattan's Upper West Side that would stand in for the film's prep school. Other scenes would be shot in New York City's Central Park, while country scenes would take place in Piermont, fifteen miles north of Manhattan. The production would move to Germany for some scenes, but none of those would feature James. That allowed him to live in Connecticut for the length of the shoot. His only perk? Train fare to get back and forth from the set.

Right from the start it was obvious to Hopkins and Tarlov that they had assembled an unusually talented and powerful group of actors. "The kids were all so mature, it was scary," says Hopkins. "Basically, they were all under twenty years old, and they were just so professional. At times you would forget that they were kids and not adults." Claire Danes, in the lead role of Daisy, convinced the director that he had been right to predict an enormous future for her. "She was amazing," says Hopkins. "Just perfect." And Jude Law "was riveting," he adds. "He was just being introduced to American audiences, but it was obvious he was going to be a star." Law would film his scenes by day, then rush downtown to appear in *Indiscretions* by night—a brutal schedule he was happy to endure for the chance to appear in his first American movie.

Jude, James, and Claire all became fast friends, despite the tension between their characters in the film. The veteran actress Jeanne Moreau, sixty-nine at the time, also got along terrifically with the young cast, savoring her moments talking craft and sharing stories with such serious budding actors.

As he had done on *Angus*, James made the most of his relatively small role. Once again, he was asked to play a slightly villainous character, someone with a polished exterior who is brimming with anger and hatred inside. And, once again, he did it so convincingly that he surprised the man who had cast him. "He totally brought new stuff to the role," says Hopkins. "He stimulated both myself and Wendy to come up with other things to have him do." Hopkins was able to make Tony even meaner toward Daisy, which in turn made Law's character Ethan seem more appealing. "James being so good an actor allowed us to make Jude less reprehensible. Now when Ethan was harsh toward Daisy it looked like he was just being influenced by this really mean kid, played by James."

The shoot lasted one month and went on without a hitch. But with each passing day, Mark Tarlov was realizing more and more that selling the movie would be an uphill battle. "This was not some big and bold and brash work about the Holocaust like *Schindler's List* or *Life Is Beautiful*," he says. "This was a subtle little story based on a wonderful little play with a bunch of wonderful performances. It seemed that the subject matter demanded more than the movie was able to do with it. And movies like this that try and carve out their own little space sometimes get overlooked."

Hopkins saw the same challenges when, after the shoot wrapped, he sat down to edit his film. But he was determined to stick to his vision for the film, and not try to turn it into something it wasn't. In the middle of the editing process, Hopkins got a call from James. "He said, 'Do you think I could just come by and see some footage?'" Hopkins recalls. "I told him I was perfectly happy to have him come by, and he did. We were cutting it in Miramax's postproduction offices in Manhattan, and James took the train in to see how the film was coming out. He's very interested in movies and how they're made."

Hopkins finished cutting the movie and turned it over to the studio. They recut it and added music to strengthen some scenes. Hopkins sat down with this reedited version and made a few more changes, after which he was basically satisfied with the movie. "It was the first movie for me and I learned a lot along the way," he says. "It's certainly not perfect. But one thing I can be really proud of is that the acting in the movie is very, very good." Mark Tarlov felt equally proud of his role in the film. "When you're able to assemble that kind of cast on a $2.5 million budget," he says, "you can be nothing but proud of the movie."

And James was delighted with his performance as well. His big scene in the movie—depicting him behaving horrifically toward Daisy—didn't make it into the final cut, but the rest of his work in the movie is impressive: assured, bold, distinctive, and genuinely frightening. Tony dislikes Jewish people without even understanding why, and James was able to play this subtle shading to his character with total authenticity. As in *Angus*, he displayed a dark side that had not been hinted at before, unleashing a shocking level of anger and hatred in his key scenes with Claire and Jude. *I Love You, I Love You Not* is indeed beautifully acted, with each actor bringing nuance and dimension to their parts.

A delightful shoot, wonderful actors, great performances—now all that remained was for the movie to find its audience. But first it had to be released, and that was delayed for months and months as the Miramax marketing department struggled to find a way to sell the film. "How do you market a movie about the Holocaust that features young kids who weren't in the Holocaust?" asks Tarlov. "It's very hard to do." Miramax assembled a lively trailer and finally released the movie on October 31, 1997, in a handful of theaters in New York and one in Los Angeles.

The result? "It made no splash," says Tarlov matter-of-factly. "Not a drop. Nothing." The movie did poor business and was soon yanked from theaters. "We had a hot actress in Claire Danes, we had Jeanne Moreau, which was a good anchor for the arts crowd, we had Jude Law, an up-and-comer, and we had James," marvels Tarlov. "And, still, nothing. But I have to say, if the movie suffered at all, it was because it was a wonderful one-act play that never really made it as a three-act film."

Critics largely agreed, though some were nastier than others. "A glorified after-school special," wrote one. "Staggering under the burden of noble intentions," wrote another. A reviewer from the *Austin Chronicle* accused the filmmakers of "troweling on enough leaden symbolism and gratuitous schmaltz to seriously undermine the tale's potential impact." Notable New York film critic Janet Maslin savaged the film from top to bottom.

But the *Los Angeles Times* gave it a glowing review, and other critics applauded its sensitivity. "It's a simple yet elegant and authentic portrayal of the delicate emotions of a delicate girl," wrote a critic for *BoxOffice Online*. Moreau and Danes were commended for their "excellent, moving performances," while movie reviewer John Hart gushed about Jude Law: "He brings such intelligence and carefully shaded ambiguity to the part that he seems irreplaceable." Once again, James was not singled out by critics, in part because his role was so small, and in part because the movie wasn't around long enough to make much of an impression on anyone.

"When the movie came out," says Tarlov, "everyone was pretty disappointed." James called Hopkins after the opening, and the two consoled each other; Hopkins advised James not to pay too much heed to the harsh reviews. By then, Hopkins knew he didn't have to worry all that much about the youngster—James was going to be fine, just like the rest of the remarkable cast of *I Love You, I Love You Not*. Claire Danes enrolled in college, but found time to shoot a lead role in *The Mod Squad*. Jude Law snagged a juicy part in the futuristic Ethan Hawke/Uma Thurman flick *Gattaca*, and an eye-catching part in the Clint Eastwood drama *Midnight in the Garden of Good and Evil*. Both Danes and Law are considered among the most accomplished, exciting, and luminous actors of their generation.

James, all of eighteen when he wrapped his second movie, decided against making the full-time move to Hollywood. Instead, he opted to enroll in college. "That surprised me," says Hopkins. "I felt he could go right into making movies as a career." Tarlov knew he'd be hearing from James again, and probably sooner than later: "The thing is,

James really wants to be an actor. He really wants to act, he enjoys it. With James, it's all very much about the work."

Indeed, filming *I Love You, I Love You Not* was a positive experience for James in many ways. Once again, he got to play a part that went against his natural personality, requiring him to stretch his talents and explore his dark side. Plus, he got to work with the great Jeanne Moreau, and just as he had done when he worked with Edward Albee, James viewed the opportunity as a terrific learning experience.

James also got his first good look at big-league movie stardom. He watched how Claire Danes, nationally known from her role on the seminal TV series *My So-Called Life*, handled her teen-queen status. Danes would walk from her trailer to the set, and large packs of starstruck adolescent girls would appear out of nowhere and sidle up to their idol. They wouldn't scream or even ask for autographs; they simply walked quietly alongside Danes. It was a strange sight and it stuck with James, but he also would remember how Danes reacted to the attention. Part of her appeal to fans was that they found her eminently approachable, and Danes did nothing to damage that reputation. In a few short years, James would become just as well known for his accessibility and his ease around his adoring faithful. Like Danes, he strikes his fans as one of them, a totally regular guy. And, like Danes, he's down-to-earth enough to not let the fame go to his head.

But first James had·to worry about class schedules and midterm exams, just like any other anxious college freshman.

CHAPTER FOUR

Drew Blue

The fall of 1995 was a wonderful time for James Van Der Beek. He was finally finished with high school, which meant, among other things, that he'd never have to wear a stuffy uniform again. He had fulfilled his most important goal and made the leap from theater to film, and all the feedback he had received on the sets of his movies confirmed that he had the goods to make it big. And he had enrolled at Drew University in New Jersey, an experience he was greatly looking forward to. All through high school he had been too dedicated to acting and too busy rehearsing to pursue a social life. Now James looked at college as a chance to sow some wild oats.

Drew University is a small, selective institution nestled on two hundred woodsy acres in the northern New Jersey town of Madison, about thirty miles from New York City. With a total enrollment of fewer than 2,500 students, it is considered one of the more challenging liberal arts universities in the country. Founded in 1928 with the goal of becoming a small and close-knit academic community for students from all over the world, it strongly encourages interaction among its diverse student body. No doubt attracted to its breathtakingly scenic campus and the casual, easygoing nature of campus life—and no doubt wishing to attend a college somewhat close to home—James settled on Drew and accepted an offer of a full scholarship. His major: English and sociology.

But James was through with being an all-work-and-no-play kind of guy. He had largely sacrificed his social life in high school so he could fully concentrate on acting; now he was ready to act more his age and go a little crazy. Reviewing the events of James's short and accomplished life, it's nearly impossible to come up with any negatives about him—he really is the boy next door, the kind of guy any girl would love to bring home to mom. But in spite of all his wonderful qualities and obvious maturity, there's no denying that James was hardly a model student at Drew.

A model student would have balanced an active social life with long hours studying in the library. James tipped the scales way in favor of partying. It's not that he spent all his time attending wild campus blowouts; that was never James's style. Instead he liked to hang out, in his room, in his friends' rooms, wherever, and just cut loose. He had a guitar and he loved strumming songs; his dorm room was plastered with posters of musical groups like the Beatles, and James would spend long hours picking and singing as if he was Paul McCartney.

One favorite pastime was zoning out in front of the TV watching *The Simpsons*. Another was inviting some friends over to his room for late-night gab sessions. Staying up to four A.M. was not uncommon; nor were early-morning trips to a nearby all-night diner. James also joined 36 Madison Avenue, a campus singing group formed in the 1980s. An all-male, thirteen-member a capella group, 36 Madison Avenue recorded a CD titled *Whoa-MadAve*, which featured cuts like "School Song" and other ditties written by members. In a photo of "The Men of 36 Madison Avenue" currently posted on Drew University's Internet site, a happy-faced, shaggy-haired James can be seen smiling in the back row, scrunched behind his crooning campus buddies.

Studying? Cracking the books? The golden boy from the honor society didn't have much time for that.

James did, however, have plenty of time to make new pals. It was at Drew that James met Sarah Suzuki, a fellow student he would later call his real-life Joey—a reference to Katie Holmes's character on *Dawson's Creek*. Joey is Dawson's best friend, his closest confidante, the one with whom he can share his deepest fears and desires. Dawson

Beek's Favorites

Favorite color: blue

Favorite city: New York

Favorite class in high school: English

Favorite book: James Joyce's *Portrait of the Artist as a Young Man*

Favorite movie: *The Shawshank Redemption*

Favorite directors: Steven Spielberg, Martin Scorsese, Oliver Stone, Stanley Kubrick

Favorite baseball team: New York Yankees

Favorite football team: Green Bay Packers

Favorite athlete: Brett Favre

Favorite season: Fall

Favorite fashion aid: a baseball cap

and Joey also had a romance on the show, something the real-life James and Sarah did not. But they did become as close as Dawson and Joey, and James spent huge chunks of his time at Drew hanging out in his dorm room with Sarah, who was, by her own admission, something of a tomboy and a good match for the athletic, introspective James.

She was also a more diligent student than her pal Beek. "James was bent on graduating without having checked a single book out of the library," Sarah told *Teen People*. "I don't understand how this boy does it—he'd get these incredible grades." Indeed, despite his mediocre attendance record at classes and his decided lack of interest in studying, James managed to make the dean's list at Drew. While most of his classmates were busy reading assigned books and writing papers on them, James liked to skip the reading part and basically just wing it. "I wrote papers on books I never read!" he admitted to *Seventeen* magazine. He got away with it by crafting wildly creative essays that had very little to do with the assigned book but that somehow managed to impress his professors.

All that free time allowed James to socialize like he never had in high school. Unlike at Cheshire Academy, where James was hardly the most popular kid around, he was quite well liked by his college classmates and, now that he is a big star, well remembered by them, too. Visitors to the Drew University site on the Internet can find a student list of the Top 10 Reasons Why We Like Drew University. Number 10 is, "The most beautiful campus in Madison, New Jersey!" Number 9 is, "The food isn't that bad." The number 1 reason is, "The girl-to-guy ratio is 62:38!!" The number 2 reason? "James Van Der Beek went here!!"

It was a fun, carefree time for James, except that he couldn't get the acting bug out of his system. During his freshman year at Drew he frequently made the thirty-minute train trip into New York City to audition for plays and movies. It's possible, however, that college life detracted from the remarkable focus that James had brought to his auditions prior to Drew. Suddenly he was not as sharp as he had been at readings, and as a result his confidence diminished. Sure, he had already done two movies and been told by countless people that he was a star in the making. Yet here he was, trudging from audition to audition, schlepping from one dingy casting office to another, juggling homework with reading scripts—basically, back to square one again. All of the good things James had allowed himself to believe would happen after *Angus* was released did not come to pass, and suddenly he was just another struggling actor pounding the pavement.

"James was having trouble getting cast and I'm not quite sure why," says his *I Love You, I Love You Not* director Billy Hopkins, who after the movie went back to being a casting director and had James in to read for several parts. "It wasn't that he wasn't auditioning, because he was taking the train trip to New York City and coming in to read. I saw him for a few parts and he almost got one that was a big role. But for some reason he just couldn't get cast. I really don't know why other directors didn't see what we saw—that this is a brilliant actor who can play good guys *and* bad guys."

For the first time, James started having doubts about the business he had chosen. For one thing, he was getting more and more frustrated with the casting process. He was tired of walking into fluorescent-lit rooms and pouring his heart out to disinterested casting directors, many of whom—unlike his big fan Billy Hopkins—would munch on sandwiches and look painfully bored during his auditions. His negative feelings may have seeped into his performances, and not surprisingly his auditions did not go well. Suddenly James found himself in an acting slump—if he had been a baseball player, he'd have been hitting .198! He asked himself if being an actor was really what he wanted out of life. For the first time, he felt like quitting.

What James really needed was a break from the frustrating grind of fruitless auditions. When he finished his freshman year at Drew, a buddy asked James if he'd like to go with him on a backpacking trip to Europe. It's a time-honored tradition among college-aged kids to strap on a bulky backpack, load up on traveler's checks, find a trusty pair of boots, and bum across Europe. Why should James deprive himself of that just because he had made a commitment to becoming an actor? After all, he hadn't signed any contract that said: You're a Serious Actor, So You Can't Indulge in Youthful High Jinks. Maybe he didn't want to be an actor, anyway. "I was unemployed and depressed [because] I'd just read an issue of *US Magazine* about these up-and-coming actors all my age," James told the magazine about that difficult time in his life. "I felt completely left in the dust."

Yet the fourth major moment in his life was about to happen—only James didn't know it at the time. All he knew was that taking a trip to Europe sounded like a lot of fun—certainly more fun than sticking around the East Coast and going to auditions.

James made a decision: Forget about acting for the moment. Who needs it? *I don't care if I ever act again,* he told himself. *I'm getting burned out by this business and I'm not even out of my teens. Why allow it to make me this miserable?* James went with his gut instinct and turned his back on his one true passion. He told his friend that he would go with him to Europe. It would turn out to be one of the key decisions in his young life.

The trip to Europe lasted six weeks and was everything James hoped it would be and more. He brought along a journal and tried to write in it every day. He read books. He stayed in cheap and dingy hostels with other teenagers from different countries. He picked up a few words in the native language of every country he visited. He was enriching himself, growing, learning. He was getting a chance to be more creative than he had at a hundred auditions. He soaked up new experiences just as he had soaked up direction from Edward Albee. "James is an observer," says Patrick Read Johnson, his *Angus* director. "He looks very carefully at what's going on in the world around him, and he sees things other people might not see. What's more, he is capable of understanding what's going on and processing it in a way that he can actually make himself feel it. He's wonderfully empathetic that way." The six-week trip to Europe was invaluable nourishment for a young soul. James felt better about everything than he had in a long, long time.

Yet, for all of his pronouncements that he was through with acting for a while, the truth is that James could not abandon his goal for even the length of his trip to Europe. When he planned his six-week journey, he budgeted enough time and money to travel to England on his way home to America. The plan was to stay in London for a while and—what else?—see some plays in the city's fabled West End theater district. Acting was in his blood, after all, and it would not be that easily shaken. James stuck to his plan and, near the end of his trip, saw a number of plays in London.

The experience totally reenergized his desire to act. His batteries had been fully recharged, and suddenly he was raring to go again. James reaffirmed the commitment he had made years ago: he was going to be an actor, whatever it took. He had released the pressure he had been feeling by taking time off from the business and basically bumming around for six weeks. Now he was back and fully rested, wiser than when he left. His trip to Europe allowed him to grow emotionally and mentally, and he had stored up new memories and emotions that he could draw on down the line.

The first thing James did after returning to Drew was change agents. He approached the woman who had submitted him for Edward Albee's *Finding the Sun* years earlier, and she agreed to represent him again. Her marching orders were clear: do whatever you have to do to get me working again.

Turning his back on acting was something of a gamble, and the gamble paid off. Within six months James had landed the biggest acting job of his life.

CHAPTER FIVE

Dawsome!

Back when thirty-two-year-old Kevin Williamson—the creator of *Dawson's Creek*—was just a gangly adolescent himself, there wasn't all that much for him to do in his hometown of Oriental, North Carolina, a pretty, slow-paced fishing community along the intercoastal waterway. He could go to the movies, or he could stay at home and watch TV, or he could just hang out with his buddies and shoot the breeze. Or, he could drive two miles to a sweet little spot where all the teenagers liked to get together and party, where a kid could sneak a smoke and a beer, or take his favorite girl for a make-out session.

The name of that spot was—you guessed it—Dawson Creek. The *real* Dawson Creek. Needless to stay, the shimmering waters of Dawson Creek stayed in Kevin Williamson's memory long after he packed his bags and left Oriental for the promise of Hollywood. Whenever he thought of the creek, he thought of his own awkward passage through the ups and downs of adolescence; he thought of all the passion and emotion he felt growing up along the creek's gentle shores. It became a powerful symbol of his bittersweet, small-town coming-of-age, an image he just couldn't shake even as a fully grown adult.

The truth is, Williamson spent much more time in front of the television than he did at Dawson Creek. He'd go to the movies, too, whenever his parents were up to taking the twenty-five-mile drive to the nearest theater. But most nights he was perfectly happy zoning out on whatever sitcom was on that night. "I grew up on television," Williamson told *TV Guide*. "I slept in front of the TV every night, on top of the remote control." His favorite show? A series called *James at 15*, about a young boy coping with the rigors of adolescence. The show only aired from 1977 to 1978, but it made a lasting impression on Williamson. He never dreamed, however, back in those lazy days, that he would one day draw inspiration from *James at 15* while putting together one of television's most groundbreaking shows for teens.

Actually, Williamson's early ambition was to be an actor. He got along well with all different kinds of students at Pamlico County High School, moving easily from crowd to crowd. And he spent a lot of time writing, for the school newspaper and for the drama club. But at East Carolina State University, Williamson made the switch from writing to acting, and, in 1987, moved to New York City to try his hand at auditioning. Four years later, he had had enough of it, and he moved again, to Los Angeles, where he happily joined the swelling ranks of aspiring screenwriters and movie wanna-bes. This time, the move felt right, and Williamson sensed he had found his calling.

He was right. One of the first screenplays he wrote, *Killing Mrs. Tingle*, dealt with Williamson's antipathy toward a particular high school teacher—a teacher who had told him he would never amount to much. Williamson exacted his revenge by writing a script about a group of students who conspire to kill their teacher. *Tingle* was optioned, and its author used the money to pay back his college loans. Kevin Williamson, screenwriter, was on his way.

Except that, after that option, things slowed to a crawl. Williamson relied on his day jobs—word processing and dog-walking—to make ends meet. He would need to write another good script, and he would need to write it fast.

Then, one night, Williamson was home alone when he noticed that a window he thought he had closed was open. He grabbed a butcher knife to investigate, all the while talking to a friend on his cell phone—a friend who teased him by bringing up horror films. That image—a terrified person looking for an intruder while on a cell phone—struck Williamson as particularly compelling. He sat down to write a horror script, drawing from his childhood fascination with creepy movies (he once sat through six straight showings of *Halloween*). Pretty soon he had another full-length screenplay to peddle.

That hip, campy horror script, which Williamson called *Scream*, was soon snapped up by Wes Craven, the director famous for bringing Freddy Krueger to life in slasher flicks like *A Nightmare on Elm Street*. Stocked with young stars like Neve Campbell and Drew Barrymore, and chock-full of big-time laughs to go with its bone-chilling scares—not to mention more gore than a surgical training film—*Scream* earned more than $100 million and became one of 1997's top films (as well as the highest-grossing horror film of all time). It was voted MTV's Best Movie of the Year in 1997, and it got Williamson a $20 million production deal with Miramax. He followed his first hit with *I Know What You Did Last Summer* (with Jennifer Love Hewitt and Sarah Michelle Gellar) and *Scream 2* (Neve Campbell again, plus Jada Pinkett)—two more blood-drenched blockbusters that established him as Hollywood's savviest writer of teenage stories (in 1997, *Entertainment Weekly* magazine named him one of the 100 Most Creative People in Entertainment). His trio of top-grossers also meant that Williamson could pretty much write his own ticket from here on in—at the very least, he'd never, ever have to walk dogs for money again.

Williamson knew he should strike while the iron was hot, and, conveniently, he had a story that he was hot to tell. It was the story of his own sweet and memorable friendship with a girl, Fannie Norwood, back in his early North Carolina days. As teenagers, they were best friends, sharing all their dreams and goals—they even slept in the same bed sometimes, though they didn't actually start dating each other until they went to college. Williamson recalled this special friendship with fondness, and thought it might make a nice springboard for a story about how teenagers grow up. Not how Hollywood thinks they grow up, but how they *really* grow up. A story about the major issues and minor hassles of being a teenager, about the longings and confusion and the fun and the misery, about sex and love and finding your place in a complicated world. About all the wonderful stuff that Williamson first experienced down on Dawson Creek.

And thus was born the seminally frank and richly entertaining TV series called *Dawson's Creek*. Williamson decided to focus on the lives of four fictional teenagers, all high school sophomores, growing up in a small Massachusetts coastal town called Capeside. Through these four characters, Williamson thought he could capture the drama of being an adolescent, not only as he

The Dope on *Dawson's*

Set in Capeside, a Massachusetts beach town

Filmed in Wilmington, North Carolina

Based on a real Dawson Creek in North Carolina

Creator: Kevin Williamson (*Scream, Scream 2*)

Producer: Columbia TriStar Television

Turned down by Fox, picked up by the WB

Debuted: January 1998

Highest rated debut in the WB's history

Seasons on air: two

Months out of the year the show films: nine

Theme song: Paula Cole's "I Don't Want to Wait"

Most loyal fan base: girls ages twelve to seventeen

remembered it, but also as it appeared to him in the turbulent 1990s. Quite frankly, Williamson thought that TV shows aimed at youngsters just weren't keeping up with the rapidly changing world confronting most real-life teens. AIDS, abortion, birth control—where was the open and dynamic discussion of these issues on TV? Why was Hollywood so intent on underestimating its teenage audience? Williamson's brainstorm was actually a simple one: don't condescend to teens, just deal with the stuff they have to deal with every day, and deal with it intelligently.

The next step was coming up with characters. He already knew that he wanted to dramatize his own relationship with his best friend Fannie, so he created the characters of Dawson and Joey. Joey is a tough-as-nails sixteen-year-old—her mother died, her father spent time in prison, and she lives with her unwed sister, her sister's boyfriend, and their baby. Through it all, Williamson imagined, Joey would remain a sweet and special girl, her spirit unbroken by the harsh hand life had dealt her. All she would need to survive is a special friend with whom to share her deepest fears and sorrows, a friend she could drop in on anytime, someone to count on when the dark clouds rolled in.

That's where Dawson Leery would come in. Dawson is Williamson as a teenager, a smart, driven, and introspective aspiring filmmaker who idolizes Steven Spielberg (indeed, Williamson had a Spielberg "thing," as he called it; he flipped out when he visited Bruce, the mechanical shark from *Jaws*, on a trip to Universal Studios early in his stay in Los Angeles). Outwardly, Dawson has everything—looks, talent, great parents, great friends. But, inside, Dawson is the most sensitive teen in Capeside. He agonizes over all of life's mysteries: love, friendship, school, sex. His head is in the stars, his heart is on his sleeve, and his bedroom window is always open—so that Joey can scale a ladder and climb through it at all hours of the night.

To this sweet story of two soul mates, Williamson added a couple of fascinating sidekicks. First, there's Pacey, Dawson's closest male pal. Pacey is the wild one, a guy who follows his instincts wherever they take him, an impulsive flirt who nevertheless has trouble scoring dates. And then there's Jen, the beautiful new girl in town, moved to Capeside from New York City, where she made some big mistakes that will follow her to her new town.

Williamson fleshed out the story line, added a few adult characters, and, together with Paul Stupin, a veteran Hollywood producer who had helped develop *Beverly Hills 90210*, took the concept for *Dawson's Creek* to the Fox network. Known for its focus on teen-oriented programming, Fox seemed the perfect place to try to sell *Dawson's Creek*. Williamson passionately pitched

James (at the 1998 Emmy Awards) almost didn't sign on for *Dawson's Creek* because he feared doing TV might not be as fulfilling as film work.

Hard to believe, but James, at twenty-two, is the oldest among his *Dawson's Creek* castmates Joshua Jackson, Katie Holmes (top row), and Michelle Williams.

She's his best friend–and sometimes girlfriend–on *Dawson's*, but Katie Holmes says in real life she and James are more like brother and sister.

James joined the gang from *Dawson's*–plus Sarah Michelle Gellar and Nicholas Brendon from *Buffy the Vampire Slayer*–for a Warner Bros. press tour in 1997.

A spiffy James showed up at the 1998 Emmy Awards in Los Angeles. This time he was just an observer, but soon his *Dawson's* work could win him his own award.

James got to hang with younger brother Jared–who he says is a phenomenal athlete–in Los Angeles in 1999. Guess good looks run in the family.

A diehard movie buff with dreams of doing Spielberg films, a bespectacled Beek took in the premiere of *The Mask of Zorro* in Los Angeles.

Never one to miss a chance to show off his sporty side, James teamed up with Michelle Williams at MTV's annual Rock 'n' Jock softball game in 1998.

© Milan Ryba/Globe Photos, Inc., 1998

© New Line Cinema/Shooting Star

Polite to a fault in real life, James convincingly played a bully with the hots for Ariana Richards (from *Jurassic Park*) in his very first movie, a dark comedy called *Angus*.

Good thing James gained 15 lbs. of muscle for *Varsity Blues:* temperatures on the Texas set reached 103 degrees and caused him to sweat off several pounds a day.

As on *Dawson's*, James is torn between blonde and brunette girlfriends in *Varsity Blues*. Looks like the brunette, Amy Smart, wins him over in the end.

Foes on film but pals off-screen, James and Jon Voight attended the premiere of *Varsity Blues.* The chance to work with Voight, James has said, was a big reason he did the movie.

James (at the premiere of *Lethal Weapon 4*) is so serious about film that Billy Hopkins, who helmed his second movie, says James would make a great director himself.

In love with acting since the age of thirteen, James just wants to keep on working and hopes his fans will follow wherever his talents may take him. That should be no problem!

his show's ideas and characters, describing how it had come from his heart, and how it would sweep America's teenagers off their feet. After all, how could it miss—a show about four smart, oversexed kids experiencing all the agony and ecstasy of being a modern teen? *Dawson's Creek* was a surefire smash!

Fox said, "Thanks, but no."

Fortunately, there was another suitor for Williamson's clever teen quartet. The WB was another fledgling network eager to duplicate Fox's success with young audiences. They snapped up *Dawson's Creek* and commissioned a pilot. Time for Williamson to dig up his dream cast.

He knew he'd need some fine young actors to pull off his subtle, angst-filled story lines. He also knew he'd probably have to go with actors a few years older than the characters they'd be portraying. For Joey, Williamson really liked Katie Holmes, the Toledo, Ohio–born daughter of a lawyer and a homemaker who made her movie debut in Ang Lee's eerily elegant drama *The Ice Storm*, opposite Tobey Maguire. Holmes went down to her basement and, with her mother's help, filmed two scenes from the *Dawson's Creek* pilot script, then sent her audition tape to Williamson. Holmes, nineteen at the time, had a delicate, graceful beauty and a fierce intelligence that struck Williamson as ideal for the precocious Joey. One down, three to go.

For Pacey, Williamson wanted someone with an easy charm who nevertheless had a strong, edgy side. He singled out Joshua Jackson, who at eighteen was a Hollywood veteran. The son of a Canadian casting director for the TV show *MacGyver*, he was nine when he landed his first part—in a commercial—and thirteen when he scored his first movie: *The Mighty Ducks*, in which he played a hockey prodigy. Jackson starred in two *Ducks* sequels, and was a poised and confident screen presence when Williamson selected him for the role of the hotheaded, rebellious Pacey.

Then there was Jennifer, the party girl, and for that role Williamson wanted someone with a youthful but sophisticated allure. Enter Michelle Williams, a remarkably mature seventeen-year-old who moved to Los Angeles—by herself—at the age of sixteen in order to chase her acting dream. With parts in the movies *Species* and *A Thousand Acres*, and on TV's *Home Improvement*, Williams brought a solid, sexy wisdom to the part of Jen, and fell neatly into place alongside Katie and Joshua.

The most crucial role, of course, was that of Dawson Leery—Kevin Williamson's alter ego. It would be a marvelous, meaty role, a part that any young actor would kill for, and Williamson knew he had to get just the right guy to execute his stylized vision. He dug in his heels and began the painstaking process of weeding through hundreds of actors in New York and Los Angeles.

James got the script for *Dawson's Creek* from his agent and read it while waiting for a train in New York's Penn Station. He had recently returned from his six-week backpacking trip through Europe, and he was hot to get his acting career up and running again. At first he wasn't all that excited about reading a TV script—he was a theater guy, a movie guy, not really a TV guy. He was the actor who couldn't land any commercials, remember? But once he started reading the script, once he grasped the complexity of the character of Dawson, he changed his mind. "Then I really wanted it so much I got really nervous," James recalled.

He prepped for the part and made his way to the *Dawson's* audition. It was one of three auditions he had that day. He read some scenes and the casting director asked if he could play the part younger. James was twenty at the time, five years Dawson's senior. But playing younger was a piece of cake to James; he spoke a little higher and sailed through the reading. He took the train back to Drew University, where that night he got a call from the casting director; they wanted him back to read again.

James took the good news in an unexpected way. He went across the hall and got hold of a friend, Amy, and told her about the callback. He also told her that he was thinking of not going back to read again. Yes, he had liked the part of Dawson, but those doubts about being a TV guy— he was feeling them again. The big drawback to a TV role, as he saw it, was agreeing to a long-term commitment, something that could trap him in a part that didn't allow him to grow. A movie was over in a couple of months, good or bad, but a TV series could stretch on for years—just ask the guy who played Gilligan if he ever got to stretch his acting muscles! James was trying to talk himself out of playing Dawson.

At the same time, he thought about his *I Love You, I Love You Not* costar Claire Danes. He knew that her TV experience in *My So-Called Life* had paved the way for her enviable movie career. Maybe it would do the same for him. After all, what were the chances that *Dawson's Creek* would last five years, if it got picked up at all? Maybe ten or thirteen episodes, tops, and then he'd be free to make movies again. James went in to read for *Dawson's* again, and before he knew it he was called to Los Angeles to read for Kevin Williamson. "When I got the call that they wanted me to audition, I reminded them that I was twenty and the character was fifteen," James told the *Edmonton Sun*. "But they said that Kevin liked my look."

Then something strange happened, something that had rarely happened to James before: he got nervous. Always a cool customer at auditions,

James was suddenly a jittery mess when he read for Williamson and other producers. Williamson wasn't alarmed; looking at this strapping young guy from Connecticut, he knew he had his Dawson. He saw in him an ideal blend of looks, charm, vulnerability, and earnestness. Still, the kid had to pull it together and convince the producers he could carry a TV show. Would he be able to do it?

Williamson took James out of the audition room and tried to calm his nerves with a pep talk. The rest was up to James. Back when he auditioned for Edward Albee, he was a picture of confidence. And when he read for Patrick Read Johnson, he blew away a roomful of cynical Hollywood types. Would he be able to rise to the challenge and stake his claim to a role he wanted badly to win?

Right there, right outside that audition room, the fifth major moment in James's life took place. He took a couple of deep breaths, marched back into the audition room, and gave Williamson everything he had. He rose to the moment and responded like the winner he is. "He came back into the room and stunned us," Williamson told *People* magazine. At that moment, he added, "We knew he was Dawson."

It was James's first-ever audition for a TV pilot, and he nailed it. He overcame his nerves, dug down deep, and nailed it.

Yet not all of *Dawson's* producers were as convinced as Williamson. Some of them "didn't think I walked into the room like a star," James recalled. One producer expressed distaste with the length of James's hair. That prompted quick action from executive producer Paul Stupin, who grabbed James, hurled him into his car, and drove him around in a desperate search for a barbershop. His locks suitably trimmed, James returned and gave it another go. After all that, some studio executives continued to resist casting him as Dawson. Finally, Williamson told *US Magazine*, he lost it. "It's gotta be this kid!" he screamed to the executives. "Nobody knows the character better than me, because it *is* me!"

James had nailed his audition, and now all objections to his appearance and demeanor had been dropped. It was official: the sophomore from Drew University was now TV's Dawson Leery.

James took a week off from school to film the pilot for *Dawson's Creek*. Williamson assembled a thirty-five-minute presentation tape to distribute to media outlets to generate buzz about his show. The episode established the frank theme and adult tone of the series, and also featured what would become a staple of the show: current, popular songs on the sound track. It also established the characters and basic setup: sexy, mysterious Jennifer Lindley arrives in Capeside and moves in right next door to Dawson Leery; she bats her eyes at him and generally disrupts the safe, platonic friendship he shares with Joey Potter. Dawson's attraction to two different women was the major story line, but Pacey's adventure raised the most eyebrows: he got romantically involved with one of his high school teachers.

Dawson Leery's defining characteristic was his intense fascination with Steven Spielberg. His room is covered with posters from all of Spielberg's movies: *E.T.*, *Jurassic Park*, *Jaws*. Like his movie idol, Dawson prefers fantasy to reality, and angrily rejects efforts by classmates to bring him down to earth. He's got his head in the clouds and he likes it there. Right away, James had a pretty good handle on that side of Dawson. "I definitely relate to my character," James once remarked. "He's a lot like I was at fifteen—innocent, idealistic, impassioned, and often clueless." Furthermore, Dawson is "prone to rejecting reality for a more romantic scenario," James explained. "He's a bit of an innocent and is frequently off in his own little world, all of which I can definitely relate to."

Besides intuitively understanding his character, James had the good fortune to get along wonderfully with Kevin Williamson. Despite the twelve-year difference in their ages, the two hit it off like old friends. James particularly liked that Williamson didn't act like some big Hollywood hotshot. Instead, he showed a willingness, even an eagerness, to involve his young actors in the

The Dawson Difference

Ways James and Dawson are the same:
- Both have dirty blond hair
- Both are crazy for Spielberg
- Both are polite and introspective
- Both are good students
- Both love sports

Ways James and Dawson are different:
- James is five years older
- James shaves
- James's parents are happily married
- James drives a Toyota 4Runner; Dawson doesn't own a car
- James didn't date in high school

collaborative process. The key to Williamson's stylized vision for *Dawson's Creek* is the incredibly sophisticated dialogue he writes for his teenage characters. The challenge for the actors is to deliver these perfectly assembled thoughts and precocious witticisms in a totally believable way. That challenge would be made even harder if, in rehearsals, Williamson demanded that the actors not stray from his scripts in the least. But, much to James's relief, that was not the case. Williamson was the first one to change a line of dialogue if it wasn't working, a gesture that gained his actors' trust and respect.

James was also completely comfortable with the sophisticated dialogue he had to deliver as Dawson. He knew that few if any teenagers anywhere actually talked like Dawson, Joey, Jen, and Pacey. But, in his estimation, that was beside the point. The characters on *Dawson's Creek* talked like every teen *wanted* to talk; they said the things all teens only wished they could have said. In that way, the series avoided the worst sin a teen-oriented series could commit: condescending to its audience. Nor was James bothered by the adult themes hinted at in the pilot, and its seeming preoccupation with sex. What Williamson was doing was simply "dealing with teenage issues," James told *Ultimate TV*. "So, in other words, sex, sex, more sex. It's honest and it's fairly responsible without being preachy."

After filming the pilot, James returned to Drew University and, once again, slipped easily into the life of a regular student. He had a lot of studying to do to make up for the week he had taken off to film *Dawson's*, but he wasn't all that worried about his grades. He knew he could cram before tests and write creative term papers and end up with excellent grades no matter how much he studied along the way. He was just gifted that way. For a long time James didn't hear a word about the exciting pilot he had filmed, the one that people were saying might finally make him a star. He had heard that line before, and he knew to take it with a grain—no, a barrel—of salt.

James more or less forgot about *Dawson's* and went on with his life. He kept going to the city for auditions and landed a part in a play called *My Marriage to Ernest Borgnine*, by Nicky Silver. He commuted back and forth to the Vineyard Theater in Manhattan, juggling his Drew studies with his homework for the play. Onstage was where he belonged, James felt. *Dawson's Creek* seemed a very distant place at that time.

Then James got the call: the show had been picked up by the WB. Very few pilots actually get picked up by networks, and here was James, in his very first pilot, on his way to national exposure. He'd have to drop out of Drew for a while. He'd have to get a place down in Wilmington, North Carolina, where the show would be filmed.

Everything was changing fast. James didn't know quite how to feel.

The *Dawson* team summoned James to attend a promotional event for the show. He was happily stunned by the news that the show was a go, but he didn't yet realize what getting picked up for a network run really meant. That changed when he walked into the hotel where the promotional event was being held. All of a sudden, he heard his own voice projecting through the room. He saw a big movie screen, on which was playing a four-minute trailer for *Dawson's Creek*. There was Katie, larger than life, and there was Joshua, and Michelle, too, and there he was, James Van Der Beek, up there on the big screen in a roomful of two thousand people, including some powerful network executives. At that moment, the enormity of what was about to happen hit James like a brick. He went to a friend's apartment and called Joshua, Katie, and Michelle. "Oh my God, you guys, you got to listen to what people are saying about this," he told them. James filled them in on the buzz: that the trailer for *Dawson's Creek* had been a big hit, and that people were wild for the show. What's more, a lot of people had seen not only the trailer but also the thirty-five-minute presentation tape, and were already predicting that *Dawson's Creek* was going to be the next big hit on TV—maybe the most exciting and groundbreaking teen series since *My So-Called Life*. This was all incredibly heady stuff for James, but he hadn't seen anything yet.

Slowly, the extent to which his life was about to change was dawning on James. Not long before, he was rushing from class to class at Drew. Now here he was, getting pats on the back from network executives. James went on a press tour for *Dawson's Creek* and was absolutely stunned to see TV critics by the dozens lining up to ask questions about the show. Press conferences were packed with all kinds of people—the hype on the series was building by the minute, and the pilot hadn't even aired on TV!

Later, James attended a *Dawson's* party at Kevin Williamson's house. Joshua was there, too, and so were Katie and Michelle. There was an atmosphere of giddy anticipation as the *Dawson's* crew discussed the remarkable word-of-mouth on their series. Everyone, it seemed, had already seen it, and that was something that James just couldn't get over. He had made two feature films that very few people had seen, but that wasn't going to be a problem with *Dawson's*. Imagine the fireworks when the show actually *airs*, he thought!

A relaxed James sat at Kevin's party, trying to soak in all the positive vibes, when all of a sudden a beautiful young woman approached him. Could it be? Yes, it was: Sarah Michelle Gellar, one of the hottest young stars on television. That's right, Buffy the Vampire Slayer was coming up to talk to

Baby James. Gellar, it turned out, had seen the pilot of *Dawson's Creek*, and she had absolutely loved it. Cool, thought James, Buffy likes my show. Even cooler, Buffy is standing here talking to me!

But the very best feedback was yet to come. Kevin Williamson told James that he had received a call from Steven Spielberg's secretary. A good chunk of the *Dawson's* pilot was dedicated to the main character's youthful obsession with Spielberg, and the director's name and likeness were used frequently on the show—all without his permission. He could have ordered the *Dawson's* producers to stop trading on his very famous name, something that would have thrown a serious wrench into production. But the call from Spielberg's secretary was not a threatening one. Spielberg had seen the pilot, and he, too, had liked it. It would be okay for the series to use his name and image; Dawson could go on idolizing the great director. Once again, James was floored by the simple fact that Steven Spielberg had called about the show. *Steven Spielberg!* James himself was a huge Spielberg fan; he had studied his movies with almost as much awe and diligence as Dawson. And now he was hearing that Spielberg had not only seen him act, but that he had liked it! How many twenty-year-old actors could say that? Seeing himself in the trailer, accepting congratulations from network executives, chatting with Sarah Michelle Gellar, and, now, hearing that Steven

Spielberg liked the show—too much! James was no longer under any delusions that *Dawson's* would be a low-key endeavor; he knew he was about to be propelled into the big time.

But James had no way of knowing just how big the big time would be.

CHAPTER SIX

The Fame Game

James had finished his freshman year at Drew and was enjoying a little time off when, in the summer of 1997, Kevin Williamson packaged his thirty-five-minute promotional tape of *Dawson's Creek* and sent it to various members of the press. It was a canny move by Williamson; he knew that the story line about Pacey engaged in a romantic affair with a forty-year-old teacher would cause a stir among critics and cultural watchdogs, many of whom would undoubtedly rip Williamson for his lack of morals.

Williamson wasn't too worried about such attacks; he was ready to defend his vision of *Dawson's Creek*, his belief that America's youngsters were far more sophisticated than they were given credit for. Today's teens have grown accustomed to edgy, honest programming, feasting on a steady diet of in-your-face drama on MTV's *The Real World*, and showing a healthy appetite for the uncensored, issue-driven realism of *Party of Five*.

Some lame sitcom like *Charles in Charge* just wasn't going to cut it among today's demanding, sophisticated teens.

Williamson had already taken a lot of heat for the shocking blood and gore in his two *Scream* movies, so he knew what to expect in the way of reaction to the content of *Dawson's*. What Williamson hoped the promotional tape would do was create an aura of excitement and expectancy around the show, a word-of-mouth buildup that would pave the way for big numbers when the show eventually debuted on the WB. It didn't even matter if most of the buzz was negative and critical, as long as critics were talking about the show. The move worked: *Dawson's Creek* was easily the most anticipated series of the year.

The series pilot, blown up to one hour, was set to air in January 1998. But the marketing machinery had kicked into overdrive weeks before that start date. The fresh, engaging faces of Joshua Jackson, Katie Holmes, Michelle Williams, and James Van Der Beek could be seen all over Los Angeles, on buses, on billboards, and even in trailers in movie theaters. It was an unusually aggressive marketing approach, evidence that the WB was determined to challenge Fox's domination in the field of teen-oriented programming. The WB Television Network, which launched in 1995, had struggled in its infancy to establish an identity. But all along it showed a willingness to take chances and run daring programs. So when Fox turned down the chance to develop *Dawson's Creek*, the WB didn't hesitate to roll the dice and take a risk. Its success with *Buffy the Vampire Slayer* paved the way for more teen-oriented shows, and suddenly the network had its identity: hip, cutting edge, youth-oriented, and full of surprises. And now, as 1998 approached, it had the most-buzzed-about show of the year: *Dawson's Creek*.

Few expenses were spared when it came to positioning the show as a must-see event. J. Crew, the clothing company, signed on as the "official wardrobe provider" for the show, and even published a winter-spring catalog that skipped clothing models and, in their place, featured the four stars of *Dawson's Creek*. There they were, four young and essentially anonymous actors, brashly modeling clothes in a popular catalog that would find its way into hundreds of thousands of mailboxes. It was a savvy cross-promotional coup that further increased the anticipatory buzz around the show.

But Team Dawson didn't stop there: they were intent on hitting teenagers where they live—the video store. Hence, promos for *Dawson's Creek* ran in Blockbuster video stores across the country, accompanied by the lilting vocals and poignant lyrics of "I Don't Want to Wait," a beautiful song performed by Paula Cole, the artist who had scored a hit with "Where Have All the Cowboys Gone?" Once again, the aggressive marketing ploy worked to perfection. It took the arresting central image of the show—Dawson Leery, in chinos and a blazer, standing in a small boat in the middle of the creek, his hands dug in his pockets and his eyes gazing expectantly, apprehensively at some distant sight—and it married it to the irresistible melody and heartfelt poetry of Paula Cole's anthem, which exhorts teens to chase their dreams and not let life pass them by. The promo became a miniature work of art unto itself, an alluring and moving encapsulation of teenage exuberance and vulnerability. It managed to communicate in a startlingly efficient way the distinct and powerful vision that Kevin Williamson had brought to *Dawson's Creek*. Even better, the series suddenly had a memorable theme song, or so viewers of the promo believed.

There was only one small problem with the marketing ploy: Paula Cole had not granted Team Dawson the right to use "I Don't Want to Wait." The premiere of the show was only days away, and suddenly it looked like it might lose its now-familiar theme song. Fortunately, the WB secured Cole's permission to use the cut in plenty of time for the show's January 1998 debut, and "I Don't Want to Wait" is still the *Dawson's Creek* song.

As the premiere date approached, the cast, crew, and creators of the series were brimming with anticipation. The feeling was that this was no ordinary TV show. One *Dawson's Creek* cast member had a unique perspective on what was happening: Mitchell Lawrence. A veteran actor who had kicked off his solid career with a bit part in *Laverne and Shirley*, Lawrence had auditioned for the part of Dawson Leery's father Mitchell—a role that eventually went to the actor John Wesley Shipp. But Lawrence was asked to shoot a smaller part in the pilot, and he agreed. He played Ben Gold, Dawson's film professor, and he did it so well that Lawrence was asked back for several more episodes.

Filming *Dawson's Creek* in those early days, Lawrence found it "very clear that something was happening, something was going on," he says. There was an electricity on the set, an awareness that the four young stars of the show were destined for public acclaim. Mitchell Lawrence had seen this kind of thing before: he has a twin brother, Matthew Lawrence, who years earlier had appeared in *Beverly Hills 90210*. "When Matthew was on that show, I got a chance to see this kind of phenomenon, where something special is happening," says Lawrence. He and his brother had watched with amazement as the young stars of *Beverly Hills 90210*—Jason Priestley, Luke Perry, Shannen Doherty—had, in the relative blink of an eye, ascended to the sort of mind-boggling stardom usually reserved for big movie stars. A public appearance by Priestley or Perry would lead to all-out pandemonium; they turned up on magazine covers, TV talk shows, feature films, everywhere. Together they attained an iconic kind of celebrity that seemed totally out of proportion to their accomplishments as actors. But that only demonstrated the enormous power of the show's target demographic: young viewers, ages fourteen to twenty-one. Clearly, thought Lawrence, the stage was set for a similar breakthrough with *Dawson's Creek*.

Fantastic buzz, great writing, and cute actors, however, are not enough to guarantee runaway success. The other essential ingredient is media saturation—the kind of push that inserts the show into the public consciousness. "The only question I had was, 'Would Warner Brothers spend the money to market it that way?'" says Lawrence. "And, early on, I could tell that they would. Warner Brothers was really behind the show. There were billboards on Sunset Boulevard, all that. They really spent the money to get the show out there." Indeed, Warner Brothers allotted some $3 million to help market the show.

Finally, after all the hype, *Dawson's Creek* premiered on the WB in January 1998. It was given the coveted nine P.M. slot on Tuesday nights, right behind *Buffy the Vampire Slayer*, the network's big hit. If it could hold on to a significant portion of *Buffy*'s audience, everything would be just swell.

Dawson's Creek did better than just hold on to

some of the Buffy crowd. In its first four weeks on the air, the show scored a 5.2 rating, which means that it was seen in more than five million homes. That made it even more popular than its lead-in, *Buffy the Vampire Slayer*. In fact, it made *Dawson's Creek* the highest-rated WB show *of all time*.

But the good news didn't stop there. The show's Neilsen figures ranked it as the number 1 TV show among girls ages twelve to seventeen, and number 4 among all teenagers. Viewership statistics showed that, on some Tuesday nights, as many as half of all female teenagers who had their TV sets turned on were watching *Dawson's Creek*. *Half of all female teens in America! Dawson's Creek* was more than just a hit—it was a bona fide blockbuster! The show's remarkable success surprised even James. "It's crazy," he told *TV Guide*. "It was just this little show we were doing . . . We never expected it to be this big."

Critics, however, quickly focused on the show's sexual content. "We get dialogue about 'sex,' 'breasts,' and 'genitalia' in the very first scene," esteemed *Washington Post* TV critic Tom Shales wrote of the pilot. "*Dawson's Creek* is a raging stream of hormones." *Entertainment Weekly*'s Ken Tucker cynically credited Kevin Williamson for "the cagey way he's found to be naughty enough for some ratings-grabbing controversy."

Another problem for critics was the incredibly sophisticated dialogue delivered by the show's teenage protagonists. All the characters were supposed to be fifteen or sixteen, and yet here they were talking like erudite thirty-year-olds. "Fasten your seat belt—it's going to be a bumpy life," one character tells Dawson, paraphrasing a line from the classic movie *All About Eve*. Ken Tucker of *Entertainment Weekly* found the notion of teenagers talking to each other in campy references from classic movies laughable. "Tone is a distinct problem in this show," Tucker wrote. "Dialogue like that is a big red warning sign that something is amiss."

These were criticisms that James, his castmates, and *Dawson's* creators would have to address over and over again in the months to come. James, in particular, was very protective of his friend Kevin Williamson's dialogue. "His characters are incredibly honest," James told *Time* magazine. "They say things teenagers are thinking but don't necessarily say, especially about sexuality." Indeed, James became convinced that the show's appeal depended on the frankness of its dialogue. He would hear from fans that the reason they liked Dawson so much was that he always expressed himself honestly and in full. He never kept anything inside, never censored himself or repressed his feelings. He was a stand-in for millions of teenagers who were unable to let their feelings out so freely.

It was precisely because the teens on *Dawson's* spoke in such a sophisticated way that the show was a major hit with real-life teens; they were responding to the fantasy element of the show, to the perfect and always clever articulation of thoughts and feelings they themselves shared but couldn't always voice with such eloquence. For parents or critics to fixate on the stylized dialogue was for them to miss the central message of *Dawson's Creek*. "Give your kids credit," James advised them in the *Orange County Register*, "because they're a lot smarter than you think they are."

The reason so many critics objected to the content and dialogue in *Dawson's Creek*, James figured, was that they were in denial about what their own kids were actually talking about. The kids on the show weren't any different from the kids watching it, who talked about sex day and night and, when they weren't talking about it, were thinking about it. The only difference was that the TV teens discussed sex in a more literate way. But to argue that the *Dawson's* gang was somehow sex-crazed or oversexed was to admit to being out of touch with America's adolescents. Maybe the dialogue on *Dawson's* was idealized and a little too smart, but the feelings it expressed were 100 percent on the nose. To not discuss sex in a frank and honest way would be to condescend to the audience, something the creators of *Dawson's Creek* were determined not to do.

James's costar Mitchell Lawrence saw things the

same way. He was not a big fan of Kevin Williamson's bloody *Scream* films, but with *Dawson's* he felt the writer had hit just the right note. "Kevin Williamson has really tapped into some stuff with this show," says Lawrence. "I remember discussing with him how kids are much more aware of things today than they were thirty years ago. And unless we adults talk about things, unless we get out there and really talk about them, we're in trouble." Lawrence has two young daughters and he frequently watches *Dawson's Creek* with them. "Watching the show has gotten us into some discussions that are very good to have," he says. "Because if they don't talk about these things with us, they're going to talk about them with someone else."

Kevin Williamson didn't mind being on the defensive about his show. He knew he was on the right track by the response he was receiving from his intended audience—"a very self-aware, pop-culture-referenced individual who grew up next to Blockbuster in the self-help, psychobabble '80s," is how he described a typical *Dawson's* viewer to *Time* magazine. Arguments that teenagers simply didn't speak with the same polish and wit that Williamson's TV teens do struck the show's creator as beside the point. Kids today "are smarter than we give them credit for," he told *TV Guide.* "And they are smarter than they have ever been." James noted that, in all the hundreds of times that he was stopped on the street by fans of the show, not once—not a single time—did anyone under twenty-one ever tell him that the dialogue was too sophisticated, or that they didn't get it. They got it because they understood the feelings behind it, and they loved the show because they felt it spoke directly to them.

For James, answering questions about the controversial nature of *Dawson's Creek* was all part of the wild ride he was taking. He was a smart kid who could handle himself around the press quite nicely, and he never had any trouble articulating Kevin Williamson's vision of the show. Nor did he take any of the criticism of the show personally, except for one review, by *Entertainment Weekly*'s Ken Tucker. The magazine's television critic, Tucker wrote a review entitled "Crippled 'Creek,'" in which he not only took swipes at the show (he gave it a letter grade of C) but also took a swipe at James. "Van Der Beek has handsome features," Tucker wrote, "attached to a face shaped like a cereal box."

James could handle criticism as well as any actor out there—he had been in two movies that were panned by critics, and he knew that negative feedback came with the territory. But this swipe seemed personal, nasty, and uncalled for. "I'm a twenty-year-old kid who's on his first TV show . . . trying to do my best," James told the *St. Louis*

Post-Dispatch. "To have people in national publications take potshots at you is really upsetting." James tried not to dwell on the crack, and he put the matter behind him quickly enough. But it left a scar, and it stripped away yet another layer of James's innocence. He was now a player in the game of show business, where everything was fair game, or so it seemed. If he was going to make it in the big leagues, he would have to steel himself to such nasty remarks. Better yet, he decided, from now on he just wasn't going to read every review of the show. Let the critics say what they want: he had a job to do, and the only reviews of his work he really cared about were the ones from his castmates and directors—and, of course, the ones from himself.

Nasty reviews aside, James was having the time of his life filming *Dawson's Creek.* The show was shot in Wilmington, North Carolina, a rural outpost thousands of miles away from Hollywood which had nevertheless become a major center for movie and TV production. At the same time, it was still a small town, not all that different from the town where James grew up. Early on in the shoot the young cast boarded at the Howard Johnson's in Wilmington, a cozy little inn that allowed the fearsome foursome to get to know each other quickly. Right away, James, Josh, Katie, and Michelle all became friends, comfortable and relaxed around each other. Not long after meeting on the

Dawson's set in Wilmington, Katie and Michelle decided to play a practical joke on their male co-stars. They locked them out of their rooms, stranding them in the hallway in only their boxer shorts. There were Josh and James, two strapping guys stripped to their boxers, with only one option if they wanted to get back into their rooms: go to the hotel lobby and get another key. Katie and Michelle savored every second of the boys' embarrassing ordeal.

Stunts like that (another time, Katie laced James's glass of Coke with salt, while the guys would often use off-color language to make shy Katie blush) made for a quick bonding process. These were four levelheaded youngsters with plenty of experience in show business; none of them was about to pull a star trip or spoil the positive feelings on the *Dawson's* set. Not even James—who, after all, played the title character—felt any obligation to set himself apart from the ensemble cast. In fact, one of the things he loved about *Dawson's Creek* was that he wasn't required to carry the show; he was only *one* of many crucial ingredients in the mix. It helped, also, that James genuinely liked his castmates. Working with them was not only going to be easy, it was going to be fun. They were four kids from different parts of the globe—one from Connecticut, one from California, one from Ohio, and one from Canada—but when they got together they clicked. On camera and off, they achieved that rare and elusive chemistry that is essential to television success.

It was particularly important that James click with Katie Holmes, who was to play his very best friend in the world. The two actors had to be able to depict an unusual intimacy, and it simply wasn't going to work if they didn't get along in real life. But James felt confident the second he laid eyes on Katie Holmes. He found her beautiful, but not in a Hollywood way. She was alluring, with a cute, crooked smile and warm, inviting eyes. After all, a talent manager had discovered her while she was at a modeling school, and she did indeed have the droopy-eyed allure of a fashion model. At the same time, she was accessible, goofy, not stuck-up in any way. It was quickly obvious that Katie was a sweet, sheltered girl from the heartland, about as far from the wise and knowing Joey as you could get. She looked like just the kind of girl a high school guy could befriend *and* want to romance at the same time.

Their first night together on the Wilmington set of *Dawson's*, James and Katie got together to feel each other out and talk about their characters. It was a great meeting, one that put both actors at ease. It wasn't that each was relieved to see that the other was cool and hip; it was that they recognized in each other a reclusive, uncool quality, a little something that made them not quite fit in. Neither one would have to put on airs to impress the other. They could just be themselves, and that would be fine. Knowing that, the challenge of bringing their characters to life seemed a whole lot easier.

The other wonderful thing for James was that filming *Dawson's* allowed him to revisit his time in high school. Back when he was fifteen, the same age as Dawson, James was nowhere near as popular or emotionally expressive as his TV alter ego. He thought of himself as a dork, and his commitment to acting put a serious crimp in his social life. He didn't have a huge circle of friends, didn't date a lot, and spent most of his time off by himself, studying or running lines or listening to Broadway show tunes. He put up walls between himself and his contemporaries, and never approached the level of candor Dawson and his buddies achieve in conversation. Frankly speaking, he was not a member of his high school's hip crowd.

Yet here he was, playing the popular Dawson Leery, getting a chance to explore situations he had purposefully avoided as a fifteen-year-old. Dawson let his feelings hang out; he didn't hold back when it came to telling his friends how he felt about them. James got a second chance to contemplate all the troublesome issues that confront teenagers on the cusp of adulthood. For James, playing Dawson Leery was like going to therapy: he got to work through his own feelings of fear and insecurity from that tricky period of his life a mere five years ago. As a twenty-year-old actor with some perspective on his own teen angst, he felt that he was able to invest his character with more emotion, make him more rounded and realistic, than if he were actually a teenager playing someone his own age. It was at once a wonderful acting challenge and a personally satisfying process for James.

Of course, there was one tiny drawback to being twenty and playing fifteen—facial hair. James has it, Dawson doesn't. As a result, James has to shave not once but *twice* every working day, in order to eliminate his five o'clock shadow and keep his face peachy smooth.

James didn't mind the shaving; he was delighted to be working on the show. Despite his early reservations about doing a TV series, by the time filming started he knew he had made the right decision. Shooting *Dawson's Creek* was a long and complicated process, with lots of intricate dialogue and subtle facial expressions to capture on film, and James and his costars routinely put in fourteen-hour days. It was the kind of grueling schedule that could have caused problems among the youthful cast, but from the beginning James, Joshua, Katie, and Michelle acted like seasoned professionals. "When I first went down to do the show, I didn't really know that much about any of them," says Mitchell Lawrence. "But I was very pleasantly surprised by the overall quality of their work.

They are all great actors. I was surprised by how assured they all were right off the bat."

One of the adjustments the four young actors had to make was getting used to the hectic pace of filming a TV show. All four had movie experience, but making movies allows for a lot more time to rehearse and prepare. Not so with a TV show. "The thing that I always have trouble with is that, in television, you just don't have any time," says Lawrence. "You rehearse a scene a couple of times, just to get a feel for it, and then you go right into it, because you have ten pages of script to shoot that day." Churning through that many pages every day requires intense concentration and focus, as well as the ability to stay loose and fresh. "James was a very hard worker," says Lawrence. "He was never nervous or anything like that. I had a bunch of scenes with him, and I was always impressed by him. I remember that we laughed a lot. In rehearsals, he's not afraid to enjoy what he's doing. There was no angst about it at all."

Life on the set of *Dawson's* was hectic and grueling for fourteen hours, then slow and relaxed during the downtime. In a way, it was good that the series wasn't being filmed in Los Angeles, where, after a long day of shooting, the temptation is to hit a few hot nightspots and blow off some steam. There *aren't* any hot nightspots in Wilmington, North Carolina. Instead, the *Dawson's* gang liked to get together after hours and hang out in a low-key local restaurant called Vinnie's. It's the kind of place where the stars could go and be treated like regular people; in fact, if they ever started acting like prima donnas, James has said, the owners of Vinnie's would "smack us upside the head."

James also relaxes in his few down hours by singing—in private and in public. In the comfort of his home he likes to take out the acoustic guitar he bought for himself after winning the lead role in *Varsity Blues* and teach himself how to play. He'll strum a few tunes and croon a few lyrics, exercising the voice that landed him roles in the musicals *Grease* and *Shenandoah*. On other occasions he'll take the stage in one of the Wilmington bars he hangs out in, grab the microphone, and let loose— really let loose—with a song. "The locals in Wilmington are probably sick of me getting up and singing," James laughingly told *Seventeen* magazine. Sometimes James will slip on his black Calvin Klein sunglasses and get behind the wheel of his green-gray Toyota 4Runner, which he likes to drive around town. Another favorite pastime is trolling the *Dawson's* set in search of any pickup basketball game he can find, or just sitting at home reading and writing—enjoying a few stolen moments of peace and quiet.

But the truth is, none of the *Dawson's* actors has all that much time to kick back and act their age. Much of their nonshooting time is spent studying

What Beek Does in His *Dawson's* Downtime

- Writes short stories
- Reads classic books
- Teaches himself to play guitar
- Shoots hoops
- Tools around in his Toyota 4Runner
- Hangs out at Vinnie's Café in Wilmington
- Sings onstage at local bars
- Decorates his loft apartment
- Signs tons of autographs
- Sleeps, sleeps, sleeps!

lines, rehearsing, or just catching up on lost sleep. It's not something that you'll ever hear James complain about, but he simply doesn't have the kind of free time that most guys his age take for granted. How many twenty-two-year-olds work seventy hours a week? And that was another reason why the cast got along so well: they were the only ones who truly understood what the others were experiencing. The isolation from friends and family, the long hours, the demands of their profession—it helped to be able to turn to each other for support and words of encouragement.

When it came time to find housing in Wilmington, James turned to one of his costars: Joshua Jackson. They were both incredibly smart guys and they got along nicely, and they especially liked to argue about current events and issues. Both were looking for apartments at the same time, and so they decided to move in together and share one nifty apartment they both liked. They were joined by a third roommate: Josh's dog.

Early on, though, it became obvious that the pairing was anything but natural. James was neat and orderly, while Josh was more free-spirited and devil-may-care. People called them the Odd Couple, a reference to the Neil Simon play about Oscar, a sloppy sportswriter who takes in his neatnik friend, Felix, as a roommate. But despite their different temperaments, James and Josh got along great, inviting friends over on weekends to watch football in their bachelor pad.

Eventually, though, James felt the urge to be out on his own and, in the spring of 1998, bought a large one-bedroom loft in Wilmington. It was a great place with a sleeping loft off to the side of the living room, but it was a place that definitely needed work; for one thing, the floors and walls were *pink*! On Saturdays, James would go to Home Depot, where he loaded up on the tools and supplies he needed. Next came the furnishings. At first, all James had in the loft was a television and an old couch, but, bit by bit, he filled it with furniture, pictures of family members, and mementos from his movies and plays. His proudest purchase: a big, comfortable, pale brown suede sofa, on which he likes to sit when he does his after-hours writing. The entire apartment is done up in soft, warm earth tones, for two reasons: one, James's favorite season is autumn, and brown colors remind him of fall in Connecticut. And, two, dark colors means James doesn't have to worry too much about stains, should they occur.

It was a perfect place for James to contemplate his increasingly complex character. The show's first season saw Dawson irritate his best friend Joey by having an affair with new-girl-in-town Jennifer. That relationship ended when Jen dumped Dawson, forcing him to realize that his feelings toward Joey were more complicated than just friendship.

In the May 1998 finale to *Dawson's* first season, it looked like Joey might be leaving Capeside for France, a development that prompted Dawson finally to act on his feelings toward Joey and give her a romantic kiss.

By the second season (which found *Dawson's Creek* in a new time slot, at eight P.M. on Wednesday nights), Dawson and Joey started dating, but before long she shocked him—and broke his heart—by dumping him. Meanwhile, Jennifer set her sights on Dawson again, putting him squarely between a girl he is clearly attracted to (Jen) and a girl he knows deep down that he loves (Joey). To complicate matters, Dawson had to deal with his heartbreak over Joey while watching her get involved with an upper-class snoot named Jack McPhee. When Dawson started filming a movie about his life in Capeside called *Creek Times*, he cast Joey in the role of a girl who gets dumped. That gave him a chance to explain to her what he was going through. "It's like someone rips your heart out of your chest and stomps all over it," Dawson, explaining the character, told Joey. Later, Dawson dropped the pretense and told Joey what was on his mind. "I've spent the last few months of my existence trying to learn how to be without you," he said. James has had to bring a real sense of longing and pain to his role, and through two seasons he has done it beautifully. His secret? Complete and total dedication to his craft, something he demonstrates on all his acting jobs. "Every role I play is challenging," James explained to *Entertainment Asylum*. "I get so into every character, I wonder if I can play anyone else."

His performance as Dawson has been so convincing and compelling that after only a few episodes of the show had aired, James became a full-fledged star. All four stars found themselves thrust into the spotlight, but most of the attention centered on the hunks, James and Josh. Of the two, James stood out because he played Dawson, the title character, and as such was the obvious actor for the media to focus on. In the space of a few short weeks, James went from total anonymity to mind-boggling fame, the kind of celebrity that made it impossible for him to walk down the street without causing a stir.

Suddenly his handsome face was all over the newsstands—there he was on the cover of a special edition of *TV Guide* (his billing: "the cute one"), on the glossy cover of *Seventeen* ("sensitive, shy, sexy"), on the oversized cover of *Interview* magazine (shot by famous fashion photographer Bruce Weber and dubbed a "New American Classic"). It would have been a strange and unsettling trip for anyone of any age, and it certainly was for James, all of twenty years old when his life completely and irrevocably changed.

How James has handled the impositions of fame reveals a lot about his character. Early on, after a few episodes had aired, it became obvious to everyone associated with *Dawson's Creek* that something special was happening, that the four young actors on the show had a shot at breakout stardom. "I knew that there was going to be something there, because my stepdaughter, who was twelve at the time, was watching the show with all her friends," says Mitchell Lawrence. "That was a pretty good sign to me that this was going to catch on. They liked both James and Josh, although my daughter was partial to Pacey because she likes dark-haired guys. But all her friends loved James."

But even before the series aired, James had one of those soul-shaking brushes with fame. He was in a stretch limousine, being whisked to a press conference for *Dawson's Creek*, when he glanced out the car window and beheld a truly remarkable sight: his own handsome face, big as the side of a house, plastered across a billboard for the show. "I started laughing," James told *People* magazine, "because I didn't know how to deal with the hype. I keep asking myself, how did I get here?"

Things only got weirder from there on in—and again, some of it happened before the series even aired. *Seventeen* magazine threw a party for the show, with the hosts for the night being James and Joshua Jackson. When the boys came out, all the young girls at the party went completely berserk, screaming and squealing and carrying on as if Brad Pitt had just walked in—even though they had never seen the show and had no idea who James and Josh were! It was a good and timely lesson for James as he headed toward his turbulent date with fame. He told the *St. Louis Post-Dispatch* that it made him realize that the squeals and adulation have very little to do "with who you are as a person."

On the Wilmington set of *Dawson's*, James had to get used to packs of local fans approaching him for autographs. He was gracious, patient, and accessible, traits he hasn't abandoned now that his fame has reached new heights. "I never once saw him shun a fan," says Mark Ellis, the football coordinator who trained James for his role in *Varsity Blues*. "If he had the time he would stick around and speak to all of them."

Yet James has never been totally comfortable with the act of signing autographs for fans. He does it when called upon, and he does it with unfailing politeness, but he admits that he is not all that outgoing in those situations. He'll flash his movie-star smile for fans, but he won't say a lot or otherwise open himself up too much. Autograph seekers think they know him because they know his character, and sometimes James even comes close to telling them that he is not Dawson, he's an actor who *plays* Dawson. But getting called by his character's name on the street is something that James had to get used to early on, and something he'll have to continue to deal with for as long as the show is on.

He also had to prepare himself for the inevitable moment when strangers recognized him in social situations. He might be at a party, chatting up a girl, when, all of a sudden, she'd realize who she was talking to and totally lose it. Questions about the show and his character would soon follow, and James would have to graciously excuse himself. He would eventually figure out that one of the quirky drawbacks of fame is that, on one level, you become the character you portray. It can be a heady, ego-boosting experience, but it can also be unsettling and frustrating. It becomes nearly impossible to discern whether someone's attention and affection are directed at you, or at the character everyone knows you as. It was a concept, James admitted, that took him a while to grasp fully and come to grips with.

But the moment when James truly realized just how famous he was came a few weeks into *Dawson's Creek*'s run. He agreed to be part of a promotional event at a Seattle convention center. He would be appearing onstage along with Alyson Hannigan and Nicholas Brendon, stars of the WB's other enormous hit, *Buffy the Vampire Slayer*. James was stunned to see a frothing crowd of five thousand screaming adolescents. When he was introduced to the crowd and came out from behind a curtain, the screaming reached a thunderous peak that nearly blew the roof off the place. Crazed fans threw trinkets up onstage, and James's autograph session—interrupted repeatedly by requests for photos—was sheer madness. Afterward, security guards were summoned to escort James, Alyson, and Nicholas out of the convention center through some underground passageways, to keep them safe from screaming fans. The three young stars laughed at the situation they found themselves in, and together launched into a rendition of "A Hard Day's Night"—the song from the Beatles movie in which the Fab Four barely escape a pack of rabid fans. If there had been any doubt in James's mind about his newfound status, the Seattle event forever eliminated it; the quiet, introspective kid from Connecticut was now a full-blown teen idol.

It is a testament to his rock-solid upbringing and unusual maturity that James has handled his sudden burst to stardom with poise, class, and just the right attitude. "I can't really go to the mall anymore," James explained to *People* magazine, by way of explaining what it's like to be a heartthrob. "But I'm not complaining. You won't hear me saying, 'Oh, I'm so famous, I just can't stand it.'" Even on the remote Texas set of *Varsity Blues*—even with his hair died jet-black to make himself look different from Dawson—James couldn't escape the aggressive glare of his fans. He was in a restaurant with his costars when someone recognized him. All of a sudden word swept through the restaurant that Dawson Leery was there! James and his pals were forced to cut their meal short and split before they were mobbed by *Dawson's* fans. James didn't let the event irritate him or sour his mood; he simply laughed it off and took it in stride.

Nor has James's rise to fame been marked by even a hint of scandal. Unlike the members of the Brat Pack in the 1980s, some of whom saw their careers derailed by drug abuse, James has been a model celebrity in every way. He has said he isn't the type to act out in public, and he has also stated that he would never do anything to damage his image or that of *Dawson's Creek*. He knows that with fame comes responsibility, and James has always been able to handle responsibility well.

Of all his many accomplishments, James's handling of his fame so easily just may be his most impressive feat of all. The key to it all is his ability to analyze a situation, break it down, and finally understand it—the very skill that makes him such a solid actor. When fame swept upon him like a tidal wave, James "enjoyed it for about two seconds before I panicked," he admitted to Albany's *Times Union*. "There's no 'off' button," he realized. "You can't jump off, so it was really scary." His response? Ever the intellectual, James examined the phenomenon of fame from every angle, and finally reached an important conclusion: it makes absolutely no sense at all. Fame is irrational, driven by forces beyond your control. As long as you don't base your opinion of yourself on its ups and downs—as long as you don't let it go to your head—you'll be okay. And that is how James is able to cope with being a teen idol. "If anything," he told the *Times Union*, "I've just kind of got to learn to enjoy it a little more."

Recreating, however, isn't really James's cup of tea. In his first hiatus from *Dawson's Creek*, he chose not to take a long vacation or bum around for the summer. Instead, he did what he loves to do most—act—in a little ol' football movie called *Varsity Blues*.

CHAPTER SEVEN

Joining the Varsity

Owen Gleiberman, *Entertainment Weekly*'s long-time film critic, knows the dangers of making bold predictions in his movie reviews. An actor he touts as the next big thing today could turn up in a career-killing stinker tomorrow. Still, he could not help himself after seeing a particular movie in January 1999. "Stardom might be defined as the ability to play someone who's too good to be true and make that person seem just typical enough to be you," he wrote in a January 22 review entitled "Team Dream." "James Van Der Beek has that skill down as if he were born to it in the slickly enjoyable *Varsity Blues*."

Gleiberman wasn't finished praising James's performance in the MTV-produced sports drama. He cited another small-town high school football film from 1983, a movie called *All the Right Moves*. He noted how the charismatic star of that low-budget movie rode its success all the way to international superstardom. That actor was none other than

Tom Cruise. And now, Gleiberman was suggesting, he had a successor: James Van Der Beek. In not so many words, Gleiberman was saying that James was the kind of intense yet accessible actor who could go on to have the same kind of film career as one of the five most bankable movie stars in the world! In only his third movie, James had moved a movie critic from a national magazine to anoint him the next Tom Cruise! His dream of becoming a top-drawer movie actor had finally come true.

But none of that was on James's mind when the first season of *Dawson's Creek* came to a close in early 1998. He knew he had only a couple of months before he'd have to get back to Wilmington, North Carolina, to start shooting the second season of *Dawson's*, which had been happily renewed by the WB. He also knew he wanted to capitalize on his *Dawson's* fame and make another movie. And he knew that he wanted to play a role that was as different from his TV character as possible, so that his fans wouldn't pigeonhole him as a sensitive, small-town dreamer.

What James didn't know when he started reading the script for a film called *Varsity Blues* was that his TV fame was not going to help him get a part in the movie; in fact, it nearly worked against him! The film's producers were intent on making one of the best football movies of all time, and their goal in casting it was to find the smartest and most capable young actors they could—not just some teen heartthrob who might help them sell a few extra tickets.

Varsity Blues is a complicated story about honor, leadership, and individuality. It concerns the West Canaan Coyotes, a tough-as-nails high school football team from a small Texas town that eats, sleeps, and bleeds high school football. The Coyotes have won twenty-two divisional titles in thirty-five years under the stewardship of their ironhanded coach, Bud Kilmer, who is viewed by the citizens of West Canaan as the closest thing they have to God. The Coyotes are poised to capture their twenty-third divisional title as Coach Kilmer drives his crack squad through another hot summer of excellence. Led by star quarterback Lance Harbor, the team looks unstoppable, a sure bet to win again—and, in West Canaan, winning is everything.

It's this last part—the concept of winning at all costs—that doesn't sit well with Jonathan Moxon, the second-string quarterback of the West Canaan Coyotes. Glued to the bench because of the stellar play of Lance Harbor, Moxon—or Mox, as he's known to his teammates—isn't nearly as driven to win as the rest of the Coyotes. For one thing, he thinks that Coach Kilmer's bullying tactics send the wrong message to his young players, many of whom gladly risk serious injury and accept shots of cortisone to keep playing, just to please their

The *Blues* Scoop

- James's third movie, his first starring role
- Filmed in Austin, Texas
- Shot from March to June of 1998
- James played Mox, a jock with the soul of a poet
- James lifted weights to gain 15 lbs. of muscle
- James rarely used a stunt double for his football scenes
- James got tackled by real football players
- Beek injuries: deep bruise on his shoulder
- Typical shooting schedule: from 5 P.M. to 5 A.M.
- Typical temperature: 100 degrees
- Movie opened in January 1999, at number 1
- Grossed nearly $50 million in five weeks

maniacal coach. For another, the independent-minded Mox is a senior who has his sights set on going to college—not some big-time football college like his father wants him to attend, but Brown University, a small, primarily academic institution where Mox can once and for all escape the win-at-all-cost mentality he has come to despise in West Canaan.

Mox need only sit through five more games—and, inevitably, another division title—to be done with football, and West Canaan, forever. Then the unthinkable happens: Lance Harbor goes down with an injury. The injury occurs after the Coyotes' enormous offensive lineman Billy Bob is sent into a game despite being groggy from a concussion he had suffered earlier. A wobbly Billy Bob lets an opposing player get by him on the line of scrimmage, and that player viciously tackles Lance Harbor. The injury is serious: Lance is out for the rest of the season. It looks like Coach Kilmer's dream of a twenty-third divisional championship is over.

Kilmer has only one option: he must let Mox quarterback his team. The problem is that Kilmer doesn't very much like Mox. He once caught him reading a Kurt Vonnegut novel on the sidelines during a game, when he should have been reading his playbook. Nor does he like the way Mox questions his authority. He despises the youngster's lack of intensity at practices, and he absolutely can't stand Mox's penchant for running his own plays instead of those his coach calls. But he has no choice; it's Mox or it's nothing. Coach Kilmer will do everything in his power to break Mox's spirit and get him to come around to his way of thinking.

Mox steps into the quarterback slot and leads his team to the championship game. He's always been a great athlete, he just never loved the game of football as much as his father, a mediocre player who served his own tour of duty under the tough Coach Kilmer. But now that Mox is suddenly the golden boy in town—admired by his father, pursued by Lance Harbor's girlfriend, courted by the media—he has a choice to make. Does he stick to his guns and renounce Coach Kilmer's harmful methods? Or does he win the championship game and further cement Coach Kilmer's standing as the pope of West Canaan? He knows that if he wins the game, Coach Kilmer will remain entrenched as coach until, one day in the not-too-distant future, he will get a chance to terrorize Mox's sweet younger brother, just as he terrorized Mox and Mox's dad. What is Mox to do?

It was an ambitiously complex coming-of-age story, and it would require a deft touch to make it work. The movie's director was Brian Robbins, who had earlier directed the lively comedy *Good Burger*. Robbins was also known as the actor who played the brainy but rebellious Eric Mardian in the ABC sitcom *Head of the Class*, which aired in the 1980s. He was eager to direct a hard-hitting, gritty movie unlike anything he had been associated with before. He settled on *Varsity Blues*, which would be produced by Marquee Tollin/Robbins, the company he had founded with his friend and partner Mike Tollin. It would be coproduced by MTV Films, which would give it instant cachet among the music channel's millions of youthful viewers. Robbins had a hot script and a cool production deal; now all he needed were the right actors to bring his vision to life.

There were several key parts to fill besides Jonathan Moxon. According to the story, Mox and four other star players on the squad had been childhood friends. One of them was the handsome and charming quarterback Lance Harbor, and for that role the producers settled on Paul Walker, a former high school football player himself. Next up was the role of Tweeder, a wide receiver and the team's wild man. Full of bravado and mischief, the part called for an intense and charismatic actor, and that's just what the producers got in Scott Caan. The juicy role of big-as-a-house Billy Bob went to the likable Ron Lester, while the part of Wendell Brown, the team's star running back, was awarded to Eliel Swinton, a total newcomer to acting; he had been working as a production assistant in Robbins's office when Brian read him for the role. One thing Swinton had working in his favor was that he had been an excellent running back at

Stanford University and had even played briefly for the Kansas City Chiefs of the National Football League. His athletic background was certainly impressive, but even more remarkable was his acting talent—Swinton was a total natural in front of the camera.

The two female leads were also crucial casting decisions. Former fashion model Amy Smart snagged the part of Mox's serious and antifootball girlfriend Jules Harbor (Lance's sister), while Smart's friend and fellow model Ali Larter slipped into the role of Darcy, the team's head cheerleader and Lance Harbor's girlfriend. Larter wound up acting in one of the most memorable scenes in *Varsity Blues*, the one in which she tries to seduce Mox wearing nothing but a whipped-cream bikini. For the part of Coach Kilmer, Robbins and crew wanted an actor of stature and authority, preferably someone whose very presence would communicate the coach's intimidating nature. They were lucky enough to sign Jon Voight, the brilliant actor who had won an Oscar and starred in some of the most memorable movies of all time.

But the most important role in *Varsity Blues* was the role of Jonathan Moxon, the moral center and focal point of the film. It was the starring role in the movie, the one with the most screen time, and the temptation was there to cast a well-known actor in the role. Yet none of the movie's creators gave in to that temptation. "Not once in this process did anyone, from the head of the studio to the film-makers, ever say, 'Hey, we need to get a TV star or a bankable star to play the role of Mox,'" says Mike Tollin, Brian Robbins's production partner. "It was always, 'Let's just get the best guy for the job.'"

Robbins and Tollin drew up a long list of actors they wanted to see for the part of Mox. The name James Van Der Beek was on that list, but it wasn't at the top or even near the top. "We knew about *Dawson's Creek* at the time," says Tollin. "I had seen one episode and I think Brian had seen a couple. We weren't really big fans of the show, so it wasn't, 'Yeah, we've got to get this guy for Mox.' It was just, 'Okay, this is one of the guys we should see.'"

It was the height of the *Dawson's Creek* frenzy, so James pretty much knew he'd at least be able to get in and read for the role. He flew out to Los Angeles for the audition and, as usual, he did the thing that gave him the best chance of making a good impression: he was himself. That James didn't come in with a movie-star attitude impressed Mike Tollin. "Here's a guy who, by the time we met him, already has his face on billboards on Sunset Boulevard," Tollin notes. "He's already been anointed the next great teen idol. And yet he showed absolutely none of that when it came time to position himself for the role. He had no attitude at all. In fact, we saw a number of people with a lower profile than James who came in with more of an attitude. This was not an actor who was resting on his laurels."

James's easy charm and lack of pretense had, once again, boosted his chances of getting a role. But Robbins and Tollin went out of their way to make sure James had what it took to play the part of Mox. They didn't want to cast him simply because he was the hot young actor of the moment. Indeed, they were very anxious to see if James could play someone who was more aggressive, and less introspective, than the character of Dawson Leery. After his first audition, Robbins and Tollin rented a copy of *Angus*, James's first movie, in which he played a mean and snobby high school football quarterback. They were looking for signs that James had dimensions beyond what they saw on *Dawson's Creek*. Watching James's short but memorable performance in *Angus* "really gave us a comfort level in our thinking about him," says Tollin. "Plus it was great to see him in a football uniform."

Tollin and Robbins called James back for another audition. James agreed to fly back from the East Coast and film a screen test for *Varsity Blues*. They had him perform the scene from *Varsity Blues* where Mox consoles an injured Billy Bob as he drunkenly shoots his old football trophies. It was a poignant and subtle scene that James performed beautifully. All in all, James auditioned three times for the part of Mox. With each passing minute they spent with James, the producers were becoming more and more convinced that he was an actor of depth and agility beyond his largely one-note role in *Dawson's Creek*. They had seen him play a viciously mean bully in *Angus*, quite a switch from the somewhat passive and always polite Dawson Leery. They were pretty sure he had the right amount of passion and honesty to do justice to the role of Mox. But they still needed to find out one more thing: could he throw a damn football?

Little did they know that before his fateful concussion, James had aspired to football glory. All the producers knew was that they didn't want to make the kind of sports movie where the camera always cuts away when the star actor throws the football. Mike Tollin, who had helped create award-winning sports documentaries, wanted to make the most authentic and believable football movie ever made, and for that he would need an actor who could really throw the football. "We were intent on making the action look real," Tollin says. "We didn't want to cut to a close-up of the ball landing in a receiver's hands. This movie was playing for keeps." After one audition, Robbins and Tollin took James out to the parking lot behind their offices, off Lankershire Drive and across the street from Rocky's Hamburger joint. They tossed James a football and said, "Let's see what you got."

James reared back and threw the football to Tollin. It was instantly obvious that the kid could throw. His motion was perfect, his arm was strong, and he looked very much like he knew what he was doing. "When James came in he had a pretty decent arm," says Mark Ellis, the football coordinator on *Varsity Blues*, and a former football player who can spot a fraud at fifty yards. "You never know what you're going to get with actors, but with James we knew that we didn't have to use a double for his throwing scenes."

The list of actors for Mox shrank from several dozen down to a handful and then down to three or four. James Van Der Beek was one of those finalists. A few weeks before production, Robbins and Tollin filmed three different actors in the role of Mox and screened the tests in a theater. They watched all three screen tests and finally reached a conclusion. "By that point it was unanimous," says Tollin. "James was Mox." Tollin stresses again that James's *Dawson's* fame played no part in his snagging the role. "This decision was really done in the right way," says Tollin. "The studio agreed that this needed to be about who's going to be the most believable, the most appealing actor. And that was James. The dynamic between him and Jon Voight was just great." Of course, adds Tollin, "The studio was thrilled when we picked James. He broadens the audience a little bit, and makes it more attractive to teenage girls, more than a regular football movie might be."

Finding a talented, captivating actor who is also a teen idol and TV star is a stroke of luck that only comes along every so often in Hollywood. "When forces conspire in your favor," says Tollin, "that's when you get a hit movie." James now had the part of Mox; little did he know what was in store for him.

Waiting for him down in Texas, where *Varsity Blues* would be filmed, was a man named Mark Ellis, the football coordinator on the film. Ellis had played college football in North Carolina, and had had several tryouts as a quarterback with professional football teams. He came very close to playing in the NFL but never quite made it. Instead, he gravitated to Hollywood, where a well-known stunt coordinator asked him for his help making a football movie. Ellis went on to choreograph the football scenes in such notable movies as *The Program*, with James Caan, *The Waterboy*, with Adam Sandler, and *Jerry Maguire*, with Tom Cruise. In *Jerry Maguire*, Ellis helped the actor Cuba Gooding Jr. convincingly portray a wide receiver. The coaching worked: Gooding won an Oscar for best supporting actor.

Robbins and Tollin hired Ellis to coordinate all the football in *Varsity Blues*. It would turn out to be the biggest job of his career. "There was a tremendous amount of football in this movie," Ellis says. "We filmed a total of thirty-three plays. The most I'd ever done before that was twenty-eight on *The Program*. Thirty-three plays is a heck of a lot of football."

But before Ellis could run any plays, he needed to find some football players. Five weeks before filming started he went down to Austin and auditioned more than four hundred football studs for parts in the movie. The casting call drew high school and college players from all over Texas—players who might have been too slow or too small to be stars at big football schools but who nevertheless had a nose and a passion for the game. Ellis put all of the players through a two-day football combine, very similar to the one used by the NFL. Players ran forty-yard dashes and went through agility drills. At the end of two days Ellis had a lean and mean team of forty players who would help make *Varsity Blues* the most believable football movie ever made.

Ellis had another job, too: take the five young male stars of the movie and make them look like all-state football players. The five principal actors—Scott Caan, Ron Lester, Eliel Swinton, Paul Walker, and James—flew down to Austin, Texas, to rehearse their parts with Robbins and train for their football scenes with Ellis. "They would rehearse in the morning, and then Brian would give them to me for a couple of hours in the afternoon," Ellis says. "I would practice with them and work with them on their basic technique and skills." When James first arrived, "Brian asked me, 'So what do you think?'" remembers Ellis. "I said, 'Yeah, this guy is going to make my job easier. He's got the presence, he's going to be fine.'"

Actually, Ellis was more than pleased with the overall athleticism of all five male leads. "They all had a lot of natural ability," he says. "They needed to be coached to look like all-state players, but they were all hungry to do the part well. They were all incredibly coachable."

Ellis worked with James on his throwing motion and on his footwork. He taught him the three-step drop-back favored by some quarterbacks, and the five-step drop favored by others. He taught him how to take a snap, and how to scan the field for receivers with his eyes, not his head. He taught him how to step up in the pocket, how to throw the ball accurately, how to shift his weight onto his front foot, and how to follow through on the throw. How to make sure he got his thumb and his elbow down on the release. How to look like a real West Canaan high school quarterback. James proved "a really quick study," Ellis says. "He's a bright kid. You tell him something once, that's enough."

When all five actors were up to speed on proper technique, it was time to throw them to the lions— namely, the forty real football players who were primed and pumped to teach the Hollywood pretty boys a Texas-style lesson. James and his costars savored the challenge, and couldn't wait to take the field with the real players. "There was a certain testosterone level at work," Mike Tollin says. "These guys wanted to go out there and be able to do their own stunts and run their own plays and really compete on the same level as these real players. So that really worked in our favor."

James, in particular, was keen on mixing it up with the football studs. "We got to put on football pads, step out on the field with a bunch of real football players and actually run plays, catch the ball, run to the end zone, get hit, and see the crowds on their feet," he said. "It was a blast."

What James didn't mention was the incredible amount of focus and dedication the role of Mox required. Before filming even started, James was up to his eyeballs in assignments. He would rehearse his lines in the morning and practice with the players in the afternoon. The producers had also enrolled James in an Austin gym, and after rehearsals and football practice he'd go to the gym and lift weights. His job was to keep his weight up and make sure the nearly unbearable Texas heat didn't cause him to lose precious pounds. He had to look the part of a beefy quarterback, and that meant he had to be ripped and muscular. All in all, James gained a remarkable fifteen pounds of muscle for his role as Mox (James's other big physical change—at the director's suggestion he dyed his blond hair jet-black, as a way to distance himself from Dawson Leery as much as possible).

Amazingly, with all that to worry about, James chose to use his free time to sneak in extra work. "A lot of times I would tell the guys, 'Hey, we're going to take the day off tomorrow,'" recalls Ellis. "And James and the others would say, 'Is it all right if we come out tomorrow and throw ourselves?'" Mike Tollin confirms that James "took the role very seriously. He really is a craftsman and he's very conscientious. It's not about, 'Okay, I'm a star, I can just fly through this role.' He really worked hard and he set a nice tone for the others in the ensemble."

Mark Ellis still marvels at the level of dedication James exhibited during the shoot. "Here he is, he's got to worry about his dialogue, he's got to worry about what his character is feeling, and at the same time he's got to worry about taking twenty-one guys up and down the football field and understanding how a play is supposed to go and how it develops and all of that—that's a heck of a lot for one guy to absorb." Nevertheless, James went above and beyond the call of duty in service to his part. Even when he wasn't shooting a scene or rehearsing his lines—time he could have used to kick back and relax—James would show up and ask Ellis if he could mix it up with the real players. "He would dress with them and practice with them,"

Ellis marvels. "He really was part of the team, no question."

As important as James's ability to dramatically deliver his lines and realistically play a quaterback was his ability to earn the trust and respect of the forty real football players. "With real players, there's always a bit of, 'How is this guy going to act?'" Ellis says. "It's up to the actors to earn their trust. And James did that immediately. If he blew a play or made a mistake, he was the first guy to blame himself and not make excuses. He'd say, 'Hey, I'll get it right next time' or 'Sorry, guys, let's do it again.' He fit in perfectly with the team on camera and off."

As he had done during the filming of *Angus*, James became a leader among his castmates. "It came naturally to him," Ellis says. "A quarterback has to step into a huddle and have everyone's eyes on him, and he has to exude leadership and authority. James did that, and the players responded to him right away."

Well, almost right away. Early on, when James lined up against a real player, he heard the player singing the words to "I Don't Want to Wait," the theme song from *Dawson's Creek*. It cracked him up and threw him off balance for a second, but James responded in just the right way—he took the ribbing good-naturedly and gave it right back. Pretty soon, James and the players became fast friends and bar buddies. "We all just bonded," he told *ET Spotlight.* "All these good old Texas boys took us out on the town and drank us under the table and kicked our asses all over the field the next day. They were really unimpressed by my sensitive portrayal of Dawson Leery."

After the training camp in Austin, the production moved to Coupland, Texas, for two weeks of filming. Then it was on to the nearby town of Elgin, which would double for the fictional town of West Canaan. James arranged to wear a football jersey with the number "4" on it, in honor of his favorite player Brett Favre, the wild and woolly quarterback for the Green Bay Packers.

One of the biggest thrills for James was meeting and getting to work with Jon Voight, the legendary actor who had starred in *Deliverance, Midnight Cowboy,* and *Runaway Train.* A commanding and powerful presence with one of the most remarkable work ethics in Hollywood, Voight showed up on the set of *Varsity Blues* and put on a clinic in professionalism and dedication. "James would tell you that working with Jon really helped him," Mike Tollin suggests. "Jon is the consummate professional. You can see how much he prepares and how intense he works and what he brings to a role."

James, as he had been in the past, was eager to learn about acting at the hands of a more experienced artist. He had made the most of similar opportunities before—after all, in his short career, he had worked with some big names: Edward Albee, George C. Scott, Kathy Bates, and Jeanne Moreau. He approached working with Jon Voight with the same humility and openness. Fortunately, Voight was incredibly generous with his time and insight, giving the young actor a "master class" in acting, as James later referred to it.

But when the cameras were rolling, Voight slipped completely into the character of Coach Kilmer. He did not hold back when it came time to get tough with young Jonathan Moxon. Voight had played similarly harsh and brutal roles opposite some other stellar young actors—Will Smith, Tom Cruise, Matt Damon—and he joked about how his career had come down to tormenting teen idols. "It's my plan of intimidation for handsome actors who are doing well," he told *People*. "I'm making the life of James Van Der Beek miserable."

That seemed true enough: in *Varsity Blues*, Coach Kilmer spends a lot of time either verbally haranguing Mox or dragging him around the playing field by his helmet. "Those scenes were real," Tollin says. "They weren't all scripted. Jon was grabbing him by the face mask and yanking him around the field, and that'll wake you up in a hurry." Despite the rough stuff, James savored every second of screen time he shared with Jon Voight, and more than managed to hold his own against the Oscar winner in their intense, face-to-face confrontations.

When filming of *Varsity Blues* began, everyone knew it was going to be a long, long summer—on many days, the temperature cracked one hundred degrees, and the brutal Texas heat regularly reduced cast and crew to one big sweaty mess. But everyone soldiered on: there was a great football movie to make. James didn't mind the heat at all; in fact, he was having a ball. More than anything, he enjoyed the physical aspects of the part. Ellis says, "We'd put a lineman on him, a guy who was 250, 260 pounds. And the play would require this linesman to wrap up James pretty good. But he was always saying, 'Hey, I'm all right, we can take this one step further.' If he had his way, he would have taken most of the hits himself. He was always champing at the bit, saying 'If you think I can do this, let me do it.'"

Still, Robbins and Ellis used a stunt double whenever the action called for a really vicious hit. That's not to say that James didn't get his share of bruises; he certainly did. The biggest one came on a tricky play midway through the film. The character of Mox has already taken over for Lance, and he's leading his team to a touchdown in an important game. When the Coyotes get near the goal line, Coach Kilmer sends in a set play, but Mox ignores it and decides to run his own play. The play calls for Mox to toss the ball to another player who then tosses it back to Mox. Mox then runs the ball into the end zone himself. "So James is going to run this play instead of letting a double do it," Ellis recalls. "I usually told my players to go at James at three-quarters speed or half speed and make the hit, and we'll do it again with a double later if we need to. Well, both James and the defensive player who was trying to tackle him got caught up in the heat of the moment. James is going right at the guy and the guy is going right at him and it was one hell of a collision. I can tell you that it was a little more than three-quarters speed!"

James had scampered toward the end zone, lowered his shoulder, dropped his helmet, and run right into the defensive player—exactly what a real quarterback would do in a real football game. "Well, these guys rocked each other and James walked away with this huge bruise on his arm," Ellis says. "The other guy outweighed James by probably twenty pounds. But the hit looked great and the shot looked great and we used it in the movie. That's really James taking the hit in that scene."

James proved his mettle in yet another key scene, one that required him to complete three passes in a row. It was late in the game and the Coyotes were running a two-minute drill, which meant they went from play to play without a huddle. The cameramen were on the field with the players, shooting the scene with handheld cameras. The idea was to shoot the scene in one long, uninterrupted shot—a strategy that would work only if James completed three passes in a row. Any error on James's part and the scene would have to be restarted from the beginning. Talk about pressure. "So James calls the plays and he gets his team to the line of scrimmage and he throws three perfect passes in a row," Ellis says proudly. "Three for three."

As filming progressed, and the blazing Texas heat continued, the cast and crew of *Varsity Blues* was undoubtedly feeling fatigued. But the atmosphere on the set was exceptionally positive, and morale could not have been higher. The schedule was particularly brutal: most of the football scenes were shot at night, which meant filming would start around five in the afternoon and continue sometimes as late as six in the morning! The actors would then try to get a few hours' sleep before getting up around noon to practice plays, run drills, and get ready for that night's shoot. It was the kind of schedule that could reduce anyone to rubble, but it never even slowed James down. "You never had to wonder if James was going to show up motivated or not," Ellis remarks. "He was always there, always motivated, always in character, always ready to go."

Some nights, the producers would invite thousands of local Elgin residents to fill the stands of the high school football stadium and act as extras in key game scenes. Those nights were among the most electric nights of filming, allowing the actors to get a real feel for what it must be like to be a high school football star in Texas. Whenever James came out onto the field to film his scenes, the crowd—mostly teenage girls—would erupt into "a full-blown movie-star welcome," says Ellis. The screams and squeals would continue until James had left the field. When shooting was interrupted by long delays, it was James who grabbed the microphone and addressed the bored locals, lest they pick up and leave and force producers to cancel the scene. Says Ellis: "Brian would ask James to speak or James would just sense it himself, and he'd go up to the mike and say, 'Thanks for coming out, we're trying to make the best football movie ever and we appreciate you being a part of it.' And the crowd would just go nuts."

Toward the end of the shoot, one key scene remained to be filmed. It was the climactic scene of the movie, in which Mox is one play away from taking the Coyotes into the end zone and winning the divisional championship. Mox calls a play named the Oop-De-Oop, a weird play that Coach Kilmer all but forbade him ever to call. Basically, it's designed to have Mox throw a pass to his wide receiver Tweeder, who catches it and quickly tosses it to Billy Bob—the gargantuan offensive linesman who is never covered by the defense simply because he doesn't look like someone who can run the ball into the end zone. The genius of the Oop-De-Oop, argues Mox, is that Billy Bob will be wide open, and will run the ball into the end zone for the winning touchdown. Mox also likes the play because it gives someone besides himself the chance to be the hero, and he is always more interested in doing the right thing than grabbing the glory.

Filming the Oop-De-Oop was going to be a technical challenge, since Robbins wanted to shoot it all in one long take. That would require split-second timing, not only by the players but by the cameramen as well. Ellis put his troops through their paces in preparation for filming, hoping beyond hope that they would be able to make it work without resorting to doubles and ruining Robbins's idea for an uninterrupted take. He had confidence in his guys, but he thought that this might be asking too much of them. He also knew that he had one thing working in his favor; his guys, particularly James, were hungry to make it work.

James was hungry for a specific reason. Just as *Dawson's Creek* had given him the chance to revisit high school and do things he had never had the nerve to do himself, filming *Varsity Blues* was giving him a chance to revisit the scene of one of his biggest disappointments: the concussion that had effectively ended his football career at age thirteen. Yes, it had been a fortuitous event, propelling him into acting, which, by now, he had realized was his true calling. But, still, it nagged at him that he had never been able to achieve glory on the football field. "James basically told me, 'Mark, this is an opportunity for me to revisit the football part of my life,'" Ellis says. "'It's a chance for me to do something that I wasn't able to do back then.'"

Not surprisingly, James approached the filming of the climactic scene with all the seriousness and focus he could muster. This was his big chance to make things right, to be the hero he had never been as a kid. When Robbins yelled the word "action," a 270-pound linesman would run right at him and try to turn him into roadkill. James had to throw a perfect pass to Scott Caan, who was playing Tweeder, before the linesman tackled him to the turf. The pass couldn't be almost perfect or close enough; it had to be right on the money, because the cameras were positioned to capture the action in a specific spot. It was the hardest football-related task James had been asked to perform during the shoot—and, as a result, it was the most pressure-filled moment of the shoot as well.

Robbins yelled action and the 270-pound linesman rushed at James. This was the moment of truth for James; sure, he could screw it up and nothing terrible would happen. Robbins would yell "cut!" and everyone would line up to try it again. But to James it was important that he nail it the first time. It was his chance to right the wrongs of the past, to finally be the football hero instead of the kid with the concussion.

James dropped back, just as Ellis had taught him to do, and caught a glimpse of Scott Caan running over the middle of the field. The humongous linesman was zoning in on him like a Mack truck. James had a second or two to throw the ball and make the play work. He brought his arm back, shifted his weight, and let it go. The instant he did he was tackled to the turf by a guy who outweighed him two pounds to one. James never even saw how the play turned out.

Mark Ellis, standing on the sidelines, saw it unfold perfectly. "James throws the ball and it's a perfect spiral, right on a rope," he says with obvious pride. "It's coming right at the camera and out of nowhere Scott Caan jumps up and catches it. The timing was absolutely perfect." Scott landed, turned around, and, just before he was tackled, pitched the ball to Ron Lester, who chugged toward the end zone, shook off several defenders, and scored the winning touchdown. "And all of that was in the first take," Ellis excitedly says. "The first take! It blew me away! We're all whooping and hollering on the sidelines. This was after midnight and James and the guys are out there playing wide-open, full-blast football! And the scene in the final version of the movie—that's the very first take we shot."

It was the sixth major moment of James's life, and—once again—he rose to the occasion. He had revisited the past and he had made it right. He was, finally, the hero. "You can teach a guy to drop back and take a snap and throw a football and all that stuff," says Mark Ellis, an unabashed James Van Der Beek fan. "But you cannot teach a guy to exude his presence as a leader on camera and off. When James stepped out on that field and in the huddle, his presence was felt. Not just as an actor, but as a leader."

Varsity Blues was released in early 1999 and surprised many Hollywood insiders by shooting to the number 1 spot in its first week. Made for only $14.5 million, it eventually raked in more than $50 million at the box office. Critics generally liked the movie, calling it a cut above standard teenage fare. *People* magazine wrote that "Van Der Beek ably exudes both smarts and sensitivity."

James already had a hit TV show. Now he had his first hit movie. Those comparisons to Tom Cruise suddenly seemed right on the mark. "James has a lot of dimension as an actor and that bodes well for the future," says Mike Tollin. And he wasn't even talking about James's completely surprising performance on *Saturday Night Live*. Handsome, talented, sexy, smart, *and* funny? Is there anything this kid can't do?

CHAPTER EIGHT

Saturday Night Special

At the ripe old age of twenty-one, James had already fulfilled nearly all of his early ambitions. He had a hit TV show and he had a hit motion picture. He had done some excellent acting in plays and worked with some incredible theater professionals. He had done musicals, he had done straight drama. He had played a romantic lead, and he had played a surly villain. He played sweet and sensitive, and he had played mean and nasty. He had stunned veteran casting directors with the range of his talent, and he had driven cynical Hollywood types to predict an unlimited future for him. About the only thing that James hadn't done was show the world his warped and twisted sense of humor.

That's right—on top of all his other attributes, James Van Der Beek is a pretty funny guy. "James has a really great sense of humor," says Mark Ellis, who worked with him on *Varsity Blues*. "Guys on the set would rib him about *Dawson's* and he would give the ribbing right back." Anyone who had worked with James knew that he wasn't like the always serious Dawson Leery. Not that he was a lampshade-on-his-head kind of guy, either, but once in a while James liked to loosen things up and get goofy.

He finally got his chance to show the world his comedy chops when the producers of *Saturday Night Live* called and asked him to host the show. They wanted him for the January 11, 1999, episode, right around the time that *Varsity Blues* would be hitting theaters. *SNL* was the venerable comedy institution that had been on the air for more than two decades. The skit show had made stars out of John Belushi, Dan Aykroyd, Bill Murray, Steve Martin, and many other comedy giants. The consensus about the show was that it had seriously declined in quality in recent years, and that its current crop of writers and performers couldn't hold a candle to the original Not Ready For Prime Time Players of the 1970s. Nevertheless, *SNL* was a steady ratings grabber that regularly defied rumors of imminent cancellation. Under the stewardship of its creator Lorne Michaels, it continued to be the most lively and relevant comedy-skit show on television, and through the years it was a home to brilliant comic actors such as Chris Farley, Martin Short, Billy Crystal, Phil Hartman, and Dana Carvey. An invitation to host the show was still considered something of a benediction; it was an affirmation of your place in the pantheon of pop culture.

James eagerly jumped at the chance to host the show. Unlike other young TV actors, James had experience in front of live audiences, and knew he could handle learning a lot of lines and performing under pressure. He knew that the show would give America a chance to see a side of him they couldn't see on *Dawson's Creek*, on which he could go whole episodes without even cracking a smile. James got permission to take a one-week break from filming *Dawson's Creek* and zipped over to 30 Rockefeller Center in midtown Manhattan, the NBC office tower where *SNL* was rehearsed and shot.

To see James on the January 11 episode of *Saturday Night Live* is to watch an actor of uncommon poise, timing, and instinct. His performance was completely assured and confident, without a slipup or any hint of nerves. The quality of the writing and comedy on the show was uneven at best, but James demonstrated a brave willingness to act completely goofy and give his all to the material.

Standing backstage in the NBC studio where *SNL* is filmed, awaiting the 11:35 P.M. start time of the show, James undoubtedly must have felt the excruciating pressure that previous hosts of the show have talked about. They watch a Tele-PrompTer on which the names of the show's

Live Guys

Characters James played on *SNL*:

- An overly exuberant actor in *Cats*!
- Chris Brubaker, nerdy spelling bee champ
- Ric, a dreamy member of 7 Degrees Celsius
- Mr. Gabriel Jacobs, a.k.a. Dog Mommy
- An obnoxious guy with a laser pointer
- A stuffy History Channel host
- Frankenteen, the perfect teen idol
- Anthony, the TV repairman

stars scroll down as announcer Don Pardo reads them off for the audience. The last name to be announced is the host of the show, and when that name appears on the TelePrompTer, the host knows that in seconds the doors will swing open and he will walk out and face a national audience of millions—live! Any little goof-up will be instantly broadcast into millions of American homes! It's enough to make any seasoned performer's knees buckle, but if James was feeling any of the pressure at that moment, he did not show even a trace of it when he galloped onstage at the beginning of the show.

James was dressed in a dark blue suit, white shirt, and dark blue tie. The in-studio audience whooped and hollered for a good twenty seconds while James, his hair blond again and in his *Dawson's* cut, smiled his megawatt smile and waved to the crowd. He looked comfortable, relaxed, and completely at ease when he began his monologue: "Thank you, wow, it's absolutely incredible to be hosting *Saturday Night Live*. Most of you probably know me from my show *Dawson's Creek*."

At the mention of his show the audience predictably broke into wild applause again. But as soon as James continued his monologue, the longtime, deep-voiced *SNL* announcer Don Pardo interrupted from offstage to say, "I love you, Dawson." James's bemused response is that it's great to see that the show appeals to different gen-

erations. But Pardo continued to lavish praise on
Beek. The audience giggled at the spectacle of
James acting embarrassed by Pardo's demonstra-
tions of affection. It went on this way for a while
until the voice of Lorne Michaels scolded Pardo
for embarrassing James. The premise of James's
monologue didn't really translate into any belly
laughs, and the skit was more weird and unsettling
than it was funny, but James held up beautifully
and set the tone for the rest of the show: this was
not some stuck-up actor who would be unwilling
to make himself look silly. This was a daring
young guy who was game for anything.

James would go on to act in eight more skits in
the next ninety minutes, none funnier than a mock
documentary about what it's like backstage at
Cats, the legendary Broadway musical that has been
running for more than eleven thousand performances. The idea was that Andrew Lloyd Webber,
the show's creator, had packaged a special-edition
tape taking fans backstage to see the cats getting
ready for the show. Not surprisingly, most of the
cats—grown actors draped head to toe in ridiculous furry costumes—looked fed up and ready to
quit. Some cats slept on sofas; others smoked ciga-
rettes and looked painfully bored. One completely
laconic cat commented on how the cast of the
show was "rotting from the inside."

Then, all of a sudden, a different kind of cat appears. It's James, in a wild cat suit and cat makeup,

prancing around as if this were his very first day with the show, which it is! James's unbridled exuberance—he suggests to some veteran cats that the cast organize a get-together during the week so they can talk about the show—proves unbearable to the other cats, who attack and beat up James in maybe the funniest moment of the entire show.

Next up for James was a skit called "National Spelling Bee Championship." James plays a nerdy student called Chris Brubaker; he's dressed in suspenders, red tie, and dark Clark Kent–style glasses, and his hair is slicked back like a little boy's. The premise of the skit is that the host of the spelling bee has lost the cards on which the words are printed, forcing him to make up words for Chris and his competitor to spell. When it's James's turn, the host gives him a made-up word—blandise— and James responds incredulously, using a hilarious lisp to make himself sound younger and nerdier. "Can you please define the word?" he demands in his lispy drawl. Later in the skit, his word is "Kevin McHale," as in the well-known former basketball player. Now James is totally suspicious. The skit drew lots of laughs and was truly entertaining, thanks in large part to James's unselfconscious portrayal of an indignant grade-school brain.

James then joined four other *SNL* actors in a fictional band called "7 Degrees Celsius." They are appearing on a mock TV show called *Teen Pulse*, and they're supposed to be a hot boy band along the lines of 'N Sync and Backstreet Boys. James plays Ric, who is described as "kitten soft, killer smile, the group's spiritual leader." He wears a bleached-blond wig and his hair flops down over his eyes. He is the first of the five to address the squealing audience, and James nicely captures the phony urban slang used by boys in teen bands. "I guess we're just trying to kick it in a real fashion, sing a slammin' tune, and hang with the big dogs on the porch!" he proclaims. Then the group gets up and sings its hit single, "Conjugate My Love." The skit was a dead-on send-up of drippingly romantic, sometimes shallow boy bands, and James got a chance to show off one of his hidden talents: a strong and beautiful singing voice that could have easily landed him in the Backstreet Boys had he pursued singing instead of acting.

James's next skit was bizarre and unfunny, something called "Dog Show." It's a cable-access-type program hosted by two weird types named Miss Colleen and David, who are surrounded by tiny dogs in silly hats. James eventually joins them in the character of a Mr. Gabriel Jacobs, who is more affectionately referred to as Dog Mommy. He wears a ridiculous orange Afro wig and a full-length orange cape, and he speaks in a strange, European accent. He holds a small schnauzer wearing a sailor's cap in his hands, and he serenades the pooch with a song about making waffles. The skit went nowhere, but once again James demonstrated a total commitment to the premise and a courageous eagerness to play completely against type.

James didn't get to do too much in his next skit, which starts with an actor impersonating crooner Harry Connick Jr. As "Harry" sits at a piano and dives into "My Funny Valentine," James and a pal—dressed like grungy teenagers and sitting in the back row of the studio audience—direct a laser dot on Harry's forehead. Soon the singer becomes aware of the dot, and stops his performance to yell at whomever is zapping him. This only eggs on a snickering James and his buddy more, and they eventually drive Harry from the stage by beaming their laser pointer toward his various body parts.

In the next skit, James transforms from a shaggy, jeans-wearing teen into a tweed jacket–wearing, professorial type to play the History Channel host of a shoddy World War II documentary in a totally unmemorable skit. But after that came the most revealing and fascinating skit of the show.

It opens with three NBC executives sitting in a conference room and discussing the fact that UPN and the WB are loaded with hit teen shows. One executive laments that UPN and the WB networks have cornered the market on kids ages ten to fourteen. But another slightly deranged executive, played by *SNL* cast member Tim Meadows, has a plan to recapture this lost teen audience. With great fanfare, he unveils—Frankenteen! From behind a wall emerges James, dressed up to look exactly like Dawson Leery, in chinos and a T-shirt under an open flannel shirt. He is attached to various electrical wires, and he has two bolts, one on either side of his neck. He is playing a cross between Dawson Leery and the monster Frankenstein, and he is the evil creation of the network executive, who admits to creating him by cloning the body of Scott Wolf, the lips of Leonardo DiCaprio, the hair of Jonathan Taylor Thomas, and the blue eyes of Zak Hanson. He calls his creation "the most perfect teen idol in the history of network television."

Sounds like typecasting. When one female executive expresses skepticism about Frankenteen's powers, the monster is ordered to "attack" her. James slips out of his wires and, arms outstretched exactly like Frankenstein, he lumbers toward the terrified executive. Then, in an instant, Natalie Imbruglia's "Torn" starts playing on the sound track and James slips into his charming, handsome Dawson Leery persona. He sheepishly tells the executive that he has been wanting to talk to her for some time, but has never found just the right moment. But now, he goes on, he can't wait any longer. He simply must admit that he is in love with her, and that he doesn't care who knows about it! Then James reaches down, takes his prey gently by the sides of her head, and plants a big, romantic kiss on her. When he pulls away, the smitten woman tells Frankenteen that she is in love with him, too!

Not bad, says another male executive, but what about the other half of the audience—the boys? Once again, Frankenteen is told to attack. He lurches toward the executive like a monster until a Green Day cut comes on. Once again he becomes "the perfect teen idol." He nervously asks the executive if he can talk to him about something serious, something that is hard for him to talk about. His parents have split up, and he doesn't have anyone in his life that he can open up to and trust. Except, he admits, for this network executive, whom he calls his best friend. James slaps his latest victim on the back and shakes his hand. The man, clearly moved, says that Frankenteen's friendship means a lot to him, too.

Convinced, the network executives cast Frankenteen in a *Dawson's Creek* parody called *Crested Butte*. All goes well as James, bolts still in his neck, charms an attractive classmate with his winning smile and easy personality. But when the girl lights up a cigarette, James reacts just like Frankenstein reacted when he saw villagers carrying torches— he goes berserk and attacks the girl, mumbling, "Fire! Fire!"

It was a brilliant and funny skit that worked because James was so willing to poke fun at his teen-idol status. He gladly flipped the script on Dawson Leery and satirized the TV teen's soulful earnestness and scary sensitivity. By doing so he was acknowledging the "monster" that he had indeed become: this "perfect teen idol" who is unleashed on audiences each week by the WB. It was a smart and canny bit of acting by James, who executed the tricky satire flawlessly.

The final skit saw James playing a thoroughly Italian TV repairman named Anthony—or, as the man whose TV is being fixed calls him, "Ant-ny." James wears a dark black wig done up like a pompadour, and he wears work clothes and a giant necklace that spells out his name. He speaks in an exaggerated Italian accent, like something out of *Goodfellas*, and he has the swagger and stare of a neighborhood tough guy down pat. When the owner of his home tries to match up Ant-ny with his strange and unmarried daughter Maria, James deflects her attentions by pledging loyalty to his girlfriend. Once again, it was a nifty turn by James, further demonstrating his comedic range and agility with accents.

The show ends with James onstage in a New York Yankee baseball jersey (number "5," for the late Joe DiMaggio, who was ailing in a hospital at the time). He is surrounded by *SNL* castmates, who hug him and congratulate him on his performance. It was a truly remarkable ninety minutes of comedy, with James hurling himself headfirst into some strange and unfamiliar territory. Yet another frontier had been conquered, another hurdle had been cleared. James had now proven he could do comedy just as well as he could sing and play straight drama.

Early in the morning on January 12 was a heady, heady time for James. He had just gone out in front of an audience of millions and, on live TV, performed flawlessly and hilariously. At the same time he had a wildly popular series on TV, and one of the top-grossing movies currently out in theaters. Standing backstage in the NBC studios in that New York Yankee jersey, he truly must have felt like a world champion himself. He must have felt like there was nothing he couldn't do, no goal he couldn't reach. The sky's the limit, he must have thought. Nothing can stop me now.

At that moment, James was not the only one who felt that the world was his for the taking.

CHAPTER NINE

The Perfect Teen Idol

It's impossible to say what direction James Van Der Beek's career will take, but it seems perfectly safe to say that he's going to be in the public radar for quite some time. In his small body of work so far—a handful of plays, three movies, a TV series, and a *Saturday Night Live* hosting gig—he has more than proven that he is not only a handsome, likable actor but also an artist of impressive range and talent. Even more important, he has demonstrated that he has the smarts and poise to handle all the adulation heaped upon him. "He really does have a good head on his shoulders," says his former *Dawson's Creek* costar Mitchell Lawrence. "Not only for the acting side of things, but for the business side, too."

Put simply, James makes excellent decisions. His latest movie is a good case in point. James has a small role in an independent movie called *Harvest*, written and directed by Stuart Burkin. Set in a Pennsylvania farming community, it concerns the tribulations of a down-on-his-luck farmer who resorts to growing marijuana in order to save his farm and his family. The actress Mary McCormack, best known for being in *Private Parts*, stars as a Drug Enforcement Agency officer who comes to understand the struggles of the farmers she is investigating. The movie debuted at the 1998 Florida Film Festival, where it was warmly received by critics. "*Harvest* delivers a good crop of filmmaking," wrote *The Slant* webzine. James's role is not large or flashy enough to net him much publicity, but *Harvest* looks like a sure critics' darling, and his participation in a gritty, topical, low-budget indie film stands in stark and flattering contrast to his involvement in the *Dawson's Creek* pop-culture phenomenon.

But it is the runaway popularity of *Dawson's Creek*, and the surprising success of *Varsity Blues*, that will guarantee James the chance to make more big movies during his breaks from the show. No doubt he is being deluged by hundreds of scripts, and he'll be able to pick and choose exactly what kind of movie he wants to do. He'll also command a salary of $2 million, his current asking price, though that figure is sure to escalate in the near future. His next movie will be a high-profile period piece called *Texas Rangers*, an action film set after the Civil War that will costar Dylan McDermott, the exciting lead actor on the hit TV show *The Practice*. *Texas Rangers*, about a ragtag group of men determined to restore law and order in post-war America, was written by John Milius, who directed *Conan the Barbarian*. It is due to be released early in the year 2000—ensuring that James Van Der Beek will kick off the millennium with a splashy, big-budget movie that is likely to heighten his already-sky-high profile. "He's off to an incredibly good start," says Mitchell Lawrence. "What's going to happen is, because he's had so much success so far, the industry will start to recognize him in a good way, and so they'll offer him projects that are good. He'll be surrounded by better actors, better writers, better directors, and he'll grow. He's in a really good cycle right now."

Patrick Read Johnson, his *Angus* director, agrees. "This is a hot time for James, a really hot time," says Johnson. "You start to believe that you're indestructible, that you can do no wrong. But it's all hype, and in order to have staying power you have to do different types of movies. He's going to get offered all these *Top Gun* type of films, slick stuff, stuff with big budgets, and he might want to do those and just bank the money. But I really hope he doesn't go right into being a Bruce Willis–style action hero. I would hate for him to get trapped in a star mode so soon. He needs to follow his heart and make daring choices."

That choice could be made for him, if George Lucas decides to offer him a role in one of his *Star Wars* prequels—a part that any actor would be crazy to turn down. The absurdly successful *Star Wars* trilogy—*Star Wars, The Empire Strikes Back*, and *The Return of the Jedi*—has spawned a multi-billion-dollar industry that is nourished by an astonishingly loyal fan base. The reservoir of hard-core fans ensures that any new *Star Wars* movie—like the first prequel, *The Phantom Menace*—will be a mind-boggling financial blockbuster. Few plans have been announced for this second prequel, although the Internet—a haven for *Star Wars* freaks—has been buzzing with one particularly tantalizing rumor: that James Van Der Beek is a strong early candidate for the coveted role of a young Anakin Skywalker in *Star Wars Episode Two*. Other names are floating around, including Sean Patrick Flannery and none other than James's *Dawson's* costar Joshua Jackson, but the Van Der Beek rumor is proving especially strong.

One *Star Wars* fan even called James's publicist to ask about the rumor; he was given a terse "no comment," which led him to believe—more than a direct "absolutely not!"—that there might be something to it. Certainly, if James were to snag the role of Anakin Skywalker—the brave knight who goes on to become the evil warlord Darth Vader—it would catapult him into a stratospheric level of international fame. "I would really love to see it," says Patrick Read Johnson, a huge *Star Wars* fan. "Some of the buzz on the Internet is from fans who say, 'Oh, no, not that *Dawson's* guy for Darth Vader.' But knowing James, knowing what he can do with his eyes, he would be perfect in the part."

One choice that James is not likely to make is to leave *Dawson's Creek* before his current multiyear contract is over. He wouldn't be the first successful TV actor to split before his contract is up, and certainly few would blame James for chasing movie stardom. But that, quite simply, doesn't seem like James's style. "I think he'll be honorable and stick it out," says Billy Hopkins, his director on *I Love You, I Love You Not*. "I think he'll be like George Clooney and not leave early." Playing Dawson Leery for three or four more years wouldn't be the worst career move he could make, insists *Varsity Blues* producer Mike Tollin. "He's probably going to be on the show for a while, but that's okay," says Tollin. "A little show called *Fresh Prince of Bel Air* wasn't a terrible springboard for a certain actor named Will Smith, was it?"

Indeed, James himself has expressed a desire to stay on *Dawson's Creek* for a while. "Honestly, right now, being in a television show offers a tremendous amount of security," James told *USA Today*. "I'm locked in on the show for three or four more years, and I'll stay as long as they'll keep me."

But once his *Dawson's* run is over, James will be free to tackle the movies full-time. And when he does, says Billy Hopkins, he should do it with an eye toward broadening his repertoire. "It's really

Bone Up on Beek!
The James Quiz

1. James's astrological sign is:
   a) Virgo b) Leo c) Pisces
2. James is: a) Scottish b) Dutch
   c) Polish
3. True or false: James's last name
   means "lover of birds"
4. James's computer is a:
   a) Macintosh b) Gateway c) IBM
5. True or false: James loves
   Valentine's Day
6. James's college major was:
   a) English b) Science c) Philosophy
7. "Beek's" other nickname is:
   a) Jimbo b) Baby James c) the
   Vanster
8. True or false: James answers all
   his fan mail
9. If James weren't an actor he'd be:
   a) a football player b) a teacher
   c) a politician
10. Does James wear boxers or
    briefs?

Answers:

1. c) Pisces
2. b) Dutch
3. False! It means "by the brook."
4. b) Gateway
5. False! He thinks it's too commercial.
6. a) English
7. b) Baby James
8. False! He tries, but there's just too much!
9. b) a teacher
10. Boxers, of course!

important that he keep stretching as an actor,"
says Hopkins. "My one concern is that, because he
plays a teen idol, he'll be afraid to do something
that is totally the opposite of that. Will he jump at
the opportunity to play someone dangerous or totally unlike Dawson? Or will he play it safe?"

Patrick Read Johnson says a good role model
for James is reigning movie heartthrob and *Titanic*
dreamboat Leonardo DiCaprio. "Leo isn't jumping into stuff, he's taking interesting, challenging
roles," says Johnson. "The movies might not be successful, but his performances are brilliant. And James
could pull that off, because his fans will follow him
through most things." Johnson feels that if James
makes it through the next few years with his head on
straight and his heart still in acting, he'll be fine.
"The parts he's played so far haven't begun to plumb
the depths of what he can do," Johnson stresses.
"When he gets into his late twenties and early thir-
ties, he could easily turn into the next Harrison Ford.
James has unlimited potential; if he makes the proper
choices, he can totally rule his world."

Keeping his head on straight doesn't seem like it
will be too much of a problem for James. So far,
it's been screwed on wonderfully tight. For instance, he hasn't let his fame turn him into some
kind of serial dater, turning up on the arm of
whichever starlet is hot that week. He has kept his
love life completely low-key, and few details about
his girlfriends have ever surfaced. Most recently he

admitted to *Seventeen* magazine that he does indeed have a girlfriend, but he refused to give her name or talk about her, beyond admitting that the St. Christopher medal he wore in one of the photographs was a gift from her to him.

What's more, James is very serious about his craft and doesn't take any of his stardom for granted. You'll never catch James being flip about acting; in fact, he even advises young fans against pursuing it. "Acting is the most unstable, unreliable, heart-wrenching career to choose," he told one fan on *E! Online*. His advice to youngsters who feel the same passion he does and follow his path into the business? "Keep your eyes and ears open. Ask questions. Learn from everyone you can."

With that kind of attitude, it's no wonder so many people are betting on James Van Der Beek. What *is* remarkable is that James has come this far and not changed all that much. He's not that different from the sweet, dyslexic kid from Connecticut who got bumped on the head and became an actor. "James is the kind of kid that, if you had a daughter, you wouldn't mind seeing him show up at the front door and pick her up," says Mark Ellis. "That's the kind of guy James is."

Patrick Read Johnson goes further: "James is a totally genuine, real guy. He's going to get his girls, he's going to get his parts, he's going to get whatever it is that he wants. But he has to not forget where he comes from. I hope he never stops being the nice, warm guy he was when he walked into the audition for his first movie and shook my hand for the first time. So far, he still is."

The question is, how long can he stay that way? All indications are that he isn't likely to lose his "boy next door" appeal anytime soon. "I'll find comfort in a song," he said to *Interview* magazine, after he was asked what makes him feel good. "I'll find it in a passage in some book. I'll find it in sharing a laugh."

James Van Der Beek really *is* the perfect teen idol.

How to Reach James

Write to:
James Van Der Beek
c/o Dawson's Creek
WB Network
4000 Warner Boulevard
Burbank, CA 91522

The Best of the Boys
by
Ellen Scordato

Thirty-five guys. All of them will make your pulse pound and your heart flutter. Now you can nab the goods on these hot, sexy hunks. You'll get the 411 on everything that matters: dream dates, pet peeves, vital stats, success stories— even love and romance. You could be the right girl for one of them. Wouldn't you love to find out?

In this irresistible collection you'll find . . .

• Ben Affleck • David Boreanaz • Kobe Bryant • Matt Damon • Leonardo DiCaprio • Jakob Dylan • Brendan Fraser • the Hanson brothers • Jonathan Jackson • Derek Jeter • Andrew Keegan • Jonny Lang • Jared Leto • Jason & Jeremy London • Mase • Ryan Phillippe • Prince William • Freddie Prinze Jr. • Puff Daddy • Brad Renfro • Alex Rodriguez • Gavin Rossdale • Darren Hayes & Daniel Jones of Savage Garden • Devon Sawa • Kelly Slater • Will Smith • Usher • James Van Der Beek • Casper Van Dien • Bryan White • Scott Wolf

Published by Ballantine Books.
Available at a bookstore near you.